ANNUAL REPORT OF THE U.S.A.
FY 2013

PRESENTED BY

INSTITUTE OF POLITICS AT HARVARD UNIVERSITY

AMERICAN EDUCATION FOUNDATION

Staff

PUBLISHER
Meredith Bagby
Executive Director, American Education Foundation

EXECUTIVE EDITOR
Daniel Backman

SENIOR EDITOR
Matt Shuham

GRAPHICS EDITOR
Ashley Chen

WRITERS
Daniel Backman
Jacob Drucker
Priyanka Menon
Matt Shuham
Henry Shull
Ross Svenson

CREATIVE/PRODUCTION
Susan Woitovich

Published by Principio Books, LLC.
14525 SW Millikan Way, #75822
Beaverton, Oregon 97005
info@principiobooks.com
www.principiobooks.com

PRINCIPIO

ISBN: 1-62908-005-5

ISBN-13: 978-1-62908-005-5

Cover photo by Ruth Tsang

TABLE OF CONTENTS

A Note on the Figures in this Report

This edition of the Annual Report of the United States of America covers the federal budget for fiscal year 2013, which lasted from October 1, 2012, to September 30, 2013. Unless indicated otherwise, all years refer to fiscal years rather than calendar years. In particular, though most federal figures are reported in terms of fiscal years, note that Social Security data are almost always denominated in calendar years.

Second, please note that throughout this report some data series are adjusted for inflation and others are not. Economists describe data that are adjusted for the natural rise of prices over time as being in "real" terms; data that are not adjusted for inflation are said to be in "nominal" terms or in "current dollars." For example, Figure 29, "Immigration Enforcement Spending (Real), 1986-2012," shows total spending on immigration law and border security enforcement of $2.1 billion in 1990. In fact, in that fiscal year, the federal government spent only $1.18 billion for these purposes. The higher number represents the higher wages for each border patrol officer, higher prices for cameras and patrol cars, etc., that the government would have to pay in 2012 to get the same amount of immigration enforcement it got in 1990. Thus, the $2.1 billion is called "real" or "2012-dollar" spending, while the $1.18 billion figure is "nominal" or "current-dollar" spending.

Finally, note that not all figures may add to stated totals due to rounding.

★

INTRODUCTION

by Daniel Backman

"Don't tell me what you value. Show me your budget, and I'll tell you what you value." — Vice President Joe Biden, 2007

Last year, the editors of the fiscal year 2012 Annual Report of the United States of America (ARUSA) wrote, "[T]he future of our country depends heavily on the budget choices made by decision-makers in the federal government." In FY 2013, it became clear that our future hinges just as greatly on the budgetary decisions our leaders refuse to make.

On March 1, 2013, federal spending for the remainder of the fiscal year automatically dropped by $85 billion as part of the 10-year, $1.2 trillion cuts known as sequestration. Yet these blunt, across-the-board cuts to programs ranging from scientific research to pre-kindergarten, military weapons purchases to disease prevention, did not occur because the majority of lawmakers or Americans wanted them. Rather, they resulted from the Budget Control Act of 2011, which included these replaceable cuts—disliked by both Democrats and Republicans—as a means of compelling Congress to agree to better deficit reduction measures in their place. But alas, deadlines came and went without a deal. After over two years of paralysis, Congress managed in December 2013 to replace approximately one third of the cuts for the next two years with an amalgam of small revenue increases and cost reductions. Larger questions of tax rates and loopholes, social insurance reform, and the appropriate size and role of government, however—the very questions sequestration was supposed to force our leaders to answer—went unanswered.

Unfortunately, this example of budgetary inaction pales in comparison to the 16-day government shutdown of October 2013. Following months of disagreement over how to spend federal dollars in fiscal year 2014, the House of Representatives and Senate failed to agree to a joint budget resolution by their October 1 deadline. In fact, Congress failed to take even the minimal step of maintaining spending at current levels until a broader deal could be reached—a move known as a "continuing resolution"—which is how it funded the government in 2013. Thus, the government went unfunded for over two weeks, at which point Congress agreed to a continuing resolution to maintain the status quo through January 15, 2014. And in the process, Congress almost missed its deadline to raise the government's borrowing authority, risking default on the national debt.

Meanwhile, necessary reforms to immigration, agriculture, and social insurance programs, all with significant consequences for the federal budget, remain stalled in partisan gridlock. With Congress' approval ratings at record lows, the values of the American people clearly do not coincide with the values expressed in the workings of our political system. The budget is the epitome of this discrepancy: it pleases no one except those few who profit off political paralysis.

Indeed, if the fiscal year 2013 budget reflects one value, it is the bipartisan preference among our elected leaders for inaction. It is a preference rooted in our leaders' lack of accountability to the people they represent, the people who want solutions, but know too little about the intricacies of budget policy to demand them.

As the writers of ARUSA 2013 quickly realized, the federal budget is an opaque and complex beast. Data and analyses are scattered throughout various government reports, many of them hundreds of pages long. Even the most conscientious, passionate voter would have to spend an inordinate number of hours to gather, read, and understand enough information about budget policy to truly hold his or her leaders accountable. Especially at a time when many Americans struggle to make ends meet, and many others find politics too distasteful to devote time to, it comes as no surprise that voters have left budget details to the gridlocked political class.

It is with these Americans in mind that we have created ARUSA FY 2013. On the following pages you will find an overview of the United States' current fiscal position, including an income statement of revenues and expenditures in the years 2011-2015. You will also find analysis of the federal debt, net interest payments, and tax revenues.

Later in the report, you will find in-depth analyses of the biggest debates in budget policy over the past year, from education to immigration, agriculture to health care, Medicare to science funding. Included are interviews with academic and policy experts from the top universities and think tanks in the country. We have also incorporated charts, graphs, and other ways of making complex budget data more accessible. And in hopes that this is just the beginning of your exploration into the trillions of dollars the federal government spends every year, we have included footnotes with links to all the original sources used.

ARUSA is a joint project of the American Education Foundation (www.americafound.org), a nonprofit organization dedicated to inspiring students of all ages to active civic engagement, and the Harvard Political Review (www.harvardpolitics.com), America's preeminent undergraduate journal of politics and public policy at Harvard University's Institute of Politics.

As members of a democracy, the federal budget is ultimately our budget. Ask yourself, after reading this report, whether that budget truly represents your values. If not, do something about it. Share this report with your friends, family, and social media networks. Do more research. Call or write your representatives. Volunteer and support the candidates you trust to advance your priorities. And consider donating to the American Education Foundation to continue our work of lifting the veil on an all-too-confusing process for the benefit of all Americans.

We hope you enjoy our work.

Daniel Backman
Executive Editor

★

AMERICA'S FINANCES: INCOME STATEMENT

TOTAL FEDERAL RECEIPTS* *(In millions of dollars)*

By Type	2011	2012	2013 estimate	2014 estimate	2015 estimate	% of Total Receipts (2013)
Individual Income Tax	$1,091,473	$1,132,206	$1,234,012	$1,383,172	$1,551,774	45.5%
%Change		3.73%	8.99%	12.09%	12.19%	
Corporate Income Tax	$181,085	$242,289	$287,716	$332,819	$376,091	10.61%
%Change		33.8%	18.75%	15.68%	13.0%	
Social Security & Retirement Payments	$818,792	$845,314	$951,093	$1,030,665	$1,084,566	35.07%
%Change		3.24%	12.51%	8.37%	5.23%	
-- On Budget	$253,004	$275,813	$277,606	$291,515	$306,310	
-- Off Budget	$565,788	$569,501	$673,487	$739,140	$778,256	
Excise Taxes	$72,381	$79,061	$85,346	$104,949	$113,939	3.15%
%Change		9.23%	7.95%	22.97%	8.57%	
Other	$139,735	$151,294	$153,878	$182,023	$205,315	5.67%
%Change		8.27%	1.71%	18.29%	12.8%	
Total Receipts	**$2,303,466**	**$2,450,164**	**$2,712,045**	**$3,033,618**	**$3,331,685**	

TOTAL FEDERAL SPENDING* *(In millions of dollars)*

By Function	2011	2012	2013 estimate	2014 estimate	2015 estimate	% of Total Spending (2013)
National Defense	$705,557	$677,856	$660,037	$626,755	$612,305	17.91%
%Change		-3.93%	-2.63%	-5.04%	-2.31%	
Social Security	$730,811	$773,290	$818,402	$865,635	$916,734	22.21%
%Change		5.81%	5.83%	5.77%	5.9%	
Income Security	$597,352	$541,344	$563,994	$541,816	$534,499	15.31%
%Change		-9.38%	4.18%	-3.93%	-1.35%	
Medicare	$485,653	$471,493	$510,544	$530,893	$543,959	13.85%
%Change		-2.92%	8.28%	3.99%	2.46%	
Health Care (includes Medicaid)	$372,504	$346,742	$371,664	$442,697	$514,058	10.09%
%Change		-6.92%	7.19%	19.11%	16.12%	
Net interest	$229,962	$220,408	$222,750	$222,887	$253,560	6.04%
%Change		-4.15%	1.06%	0.06%	13.76%	
Education, Training, Employment & Social Services	$101,233	$90,823	$84,555	$129,041	$106,476	2.29%
%Change		-10.28%	-6.90%	52.61%	-17.49%	
Veterans Benefits and Services	$127,189	$124,595	$139,568	$148,222	$157,055	3.79%
%Change		-2.04%	12.02%	6.2%	5.96%	
Transportation	$92,966	$93,019	$94,486	$103,839	$115,804	2.56%
Administration of Justice	$56,056	$56,277	$60,580	$58,737	$58,951	1.64%
International Affairs	$45,685	$47,189	$56,929	$55,883	$53,861	1.54%
Natural Resources & Environment	$45,470	$41,628	$37,660	$40,156	$40,767	1.02%
General Science, Space & Technology	$29,466	$29,060	$30,734	$30,157	$30,604	0.83%
Community & Regional Development	$23,883	$25,132	$37,998	$34,663	$33,846	1.03%
General Government	$27,476	$28,036	$30,469	$28,949	$29,889	0.83%
Agriculture	$20,662	$17,791	$27,049	$23,454	$16,665	0.73%
Energy	$12,174	$23,270	$15,101	$12,680	$10,725	0.41%
Offsetting Receipts & Allowances	-$88,767	-$103,536	-$95,306	-$88,531	-$80,838	
Total, Federal Outlays	**$3,603,059**	**$3,537,127**	**$3,684,947**	**$3,777,807**	**$3,908,157**	
Total Deficit (Receipts - Spending)	**-$1,299,593**	**-$1,086,963**	**-$972,902**	**-$744,189**	**-$576,472**	

*Based on the White House FY 2014 budget.

AMERICA'S FINANCES: FEDERAL DEFICIT AND DEBT

by Henry Shull

WHAT IS THE DEBT?

Government debt is a measure of how much money the government owes to its creditors.

In most cases, the government owes money to external creditors. For example, if the U.S. federal government signs a contract with Boeing, promising to pay $2 billion in exchange for a squadron of fighter jets, then $2 billion is added to the measure of federal debt until the U.S. government has sent Boeing payment for the jets and settled the contractual obligation. This kind of debt is known as debt held by the public.

However, the government can also owe money to itself. In the case of intra-governmental holdings, one part of the government has borrowed money from another part of the government, and the amount borrowed contributes to the overall measure of federal debt until it is repaid. For example, parts of the U.S. federal government often borrow from the Medicare or Medicaid trust funds, which currently have more money than needed for payments. However, these trust fund balances must be replenished, creating an obligation on the parts of the federal government that borrow from them.

The overall federal debt, known as total public debt outstanding, is calculated by adding together the debt held by the public and the amount of intra-governmental holdings.

In contrast to debt, the government's annual surplus or deficit is a relative measure of revenue and expenditures in a given year. If the government takes in more money through taxes than it spends in a given year, the government runs a surplus. If, however, it makes less than it spends, it runs a deficit.

Economists call measures like annual deficit or surplus a flow variable. These variables express the change in a quantity's value over time. In contrast, measures that express a quantity's value at any single point in time, like the overall federal debt, are known as stock variables.

A related concept in the United States is the federal debt limit, also known as the debt ceiling. This is a limit imposed by Congress on how much debt the federal government can incur; in other words, it is a cap on how much the government can take out in loans. The debt limit was introduced in a limited form in 1917, and it took its contemporary shape in 1939. Recently, there have been heated debates in Congress related to the debt limit, with Republicans generally arguing that the government spends too much money and that the debt limit should be kept in place. In reality, though, the debt limit has been modified over 90 times since 1940, and Congress itself authorizes the spending that creates the need to raise the debt limit.

DEFICITS, SURPLUSES, AND THE DEBT IN RECENT HISTORY

Under Bill Clinton, the U.S. began to have a yearly spending surplus rather than deficit. Largely because of the leadership of President Clinton and his secretary of the treasury, Robert Rubin, the federal government accrued more in receipts than in outlays from FY 1998 to FY 2001. (These were the first surpluses since 1969.) As a result, debt decreased as a percentage of GDP. At the end of FY 1991 the ratio of gross federal debt to GDP was 60.7 percent, and at the end of FY 2001 that number had dropped to 56.4 percent.

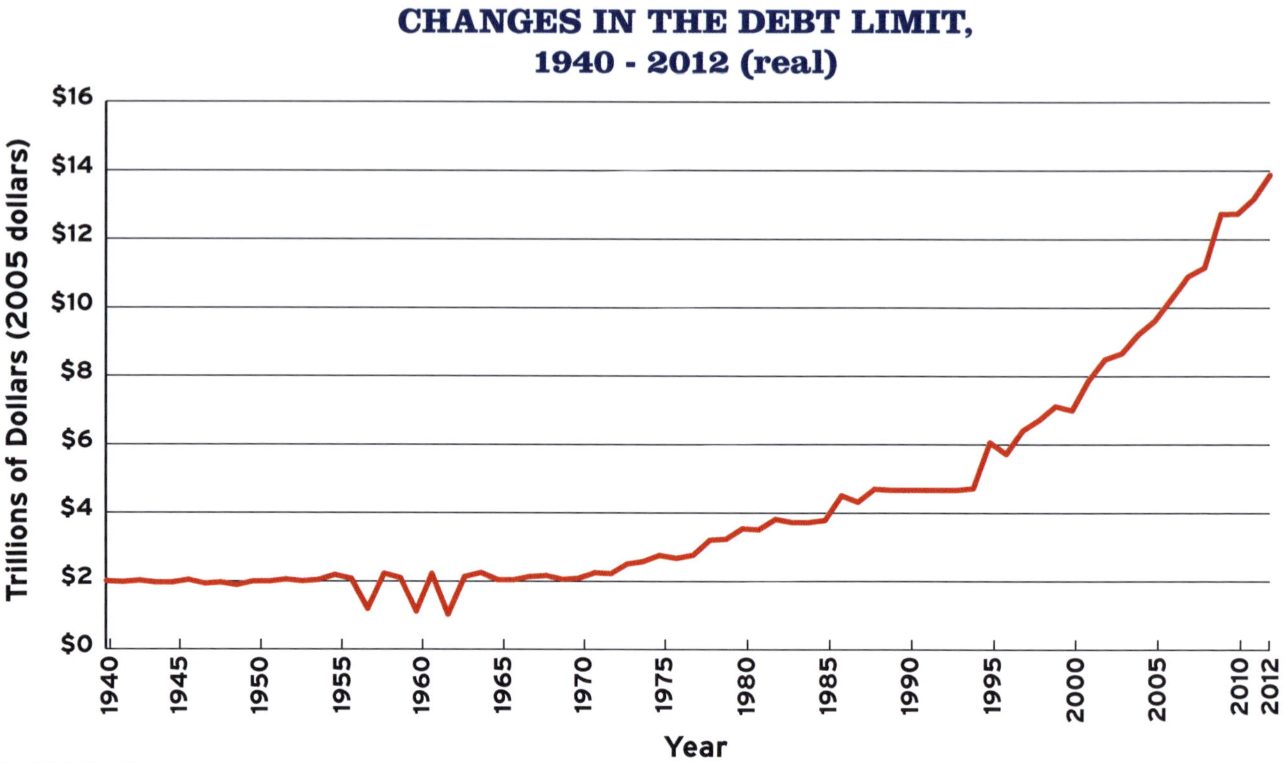

FIGURE 1 SOURCE: Budget of the U.S. Government FY 2013, http://www.gpo.gov/fdsys/pkg/BUDGET-2013-TAB/xls/BUDGET-2013-TAB-7-3.xls.

President George W. Bush's administration reversed this trend. Bush came into office with a relatively weak economy, largely a result of the dot-com bubble and the precipitous drops in economic activity following the September 11, 2001, terrorist attacks. As president, Bush decreased government revenue through a series of tax cuts, and he simultaneously increased government spending substantially through wars in Afghanistan and in Iraq and through a new Medicare prescription drug benefit plan, Part D.

At the end of the Bush administration and the beginning of the Obama administration, the government spent very large amounts of money on stimulus packages, ranging from "bailouts" of U.S. banks and automobile manufacturers to infrastructure improvements. These payments were meant to help the U.S. economy recover from the housing crisis and subsequent economic collapse that began in late 2007 and reached its nadir in late 2008.

As a consequence of all these factors, from FY 2001 to FY 2009, the gross debt-to-GDP ratio increased from 56.4 percent to 85.2 percent.

FEDERAL RECEIPTS AND OUTLAYS, 1940 - 2012 (% of GDP)

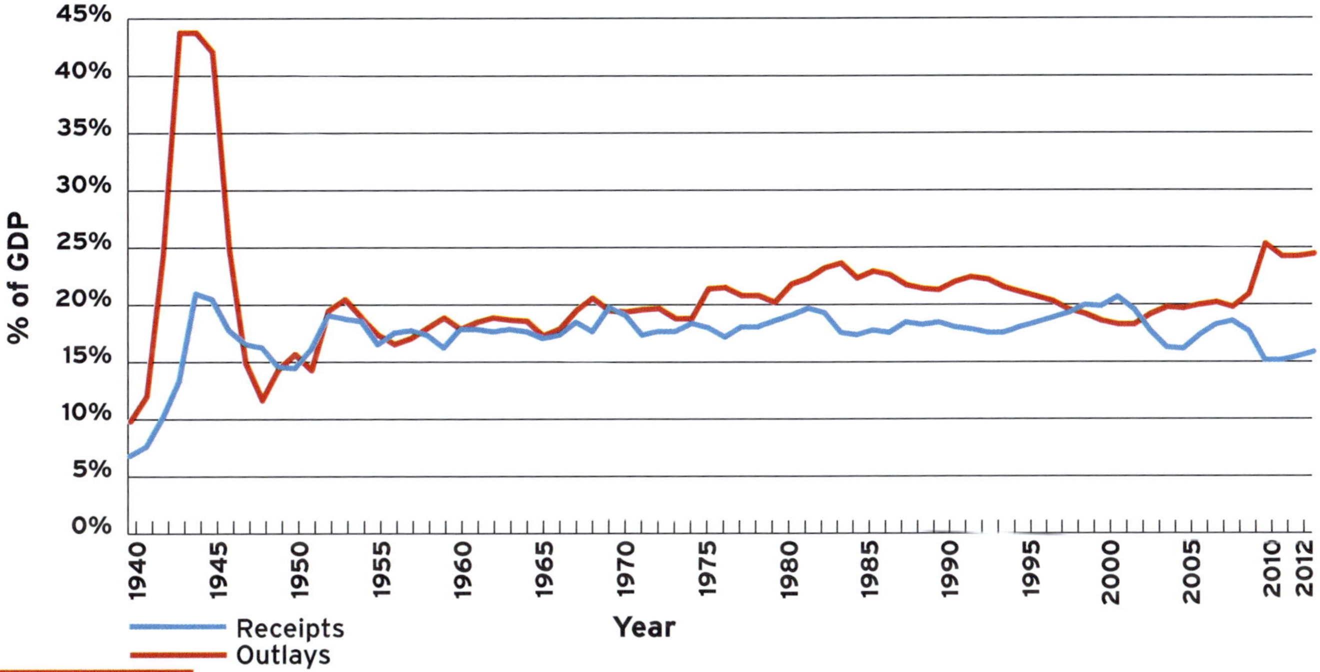

FIGURE 2

SOURCE: Budget of the U.S. Government FY 2013, http://www.gpo.gov/fdsys/pkg/BUDGET-2013-TAB/xls/BUDGET-2013-TAB-1-3.xls.

FEDERAL SURPLUS/DEFICIT, 1940 - 2012 (% of GDP)

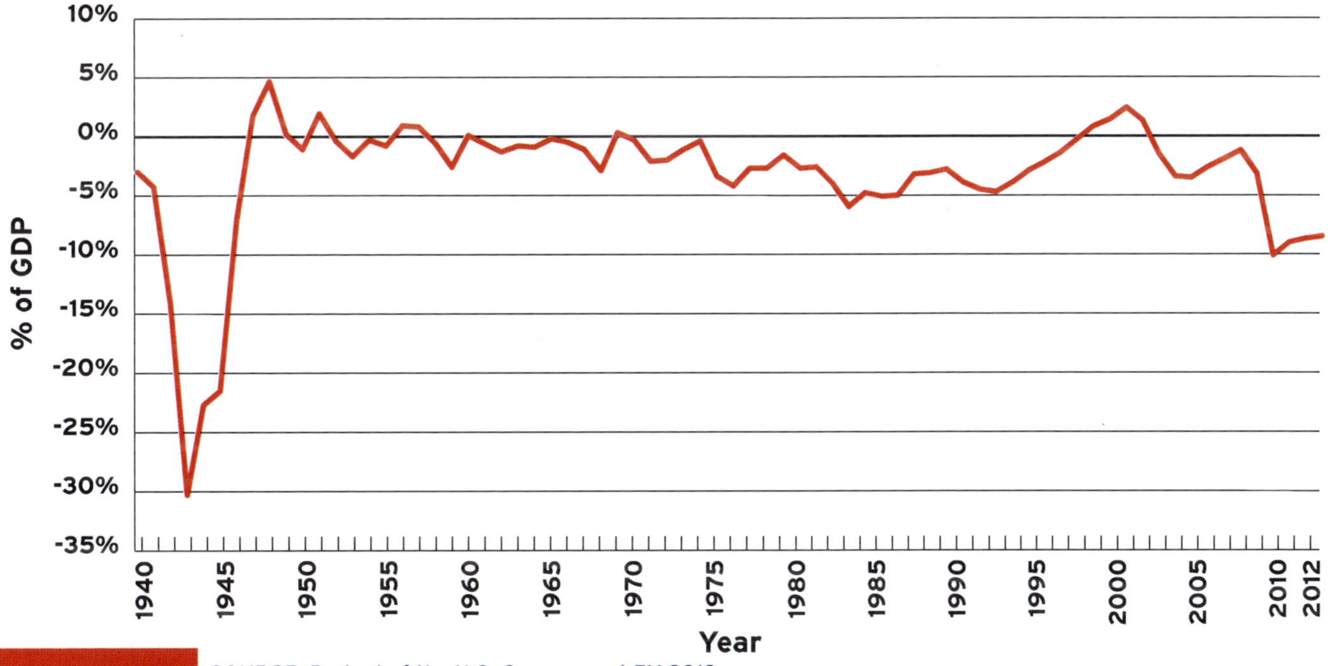

FIGURE 3

SOURCE: Budget of the U.S. Government FY 2013, http://www.gpo.gov/fdsys/pkg/BUDGET-2013-TAB/xls/BUDGET-2013-TAB-1-3.xls.

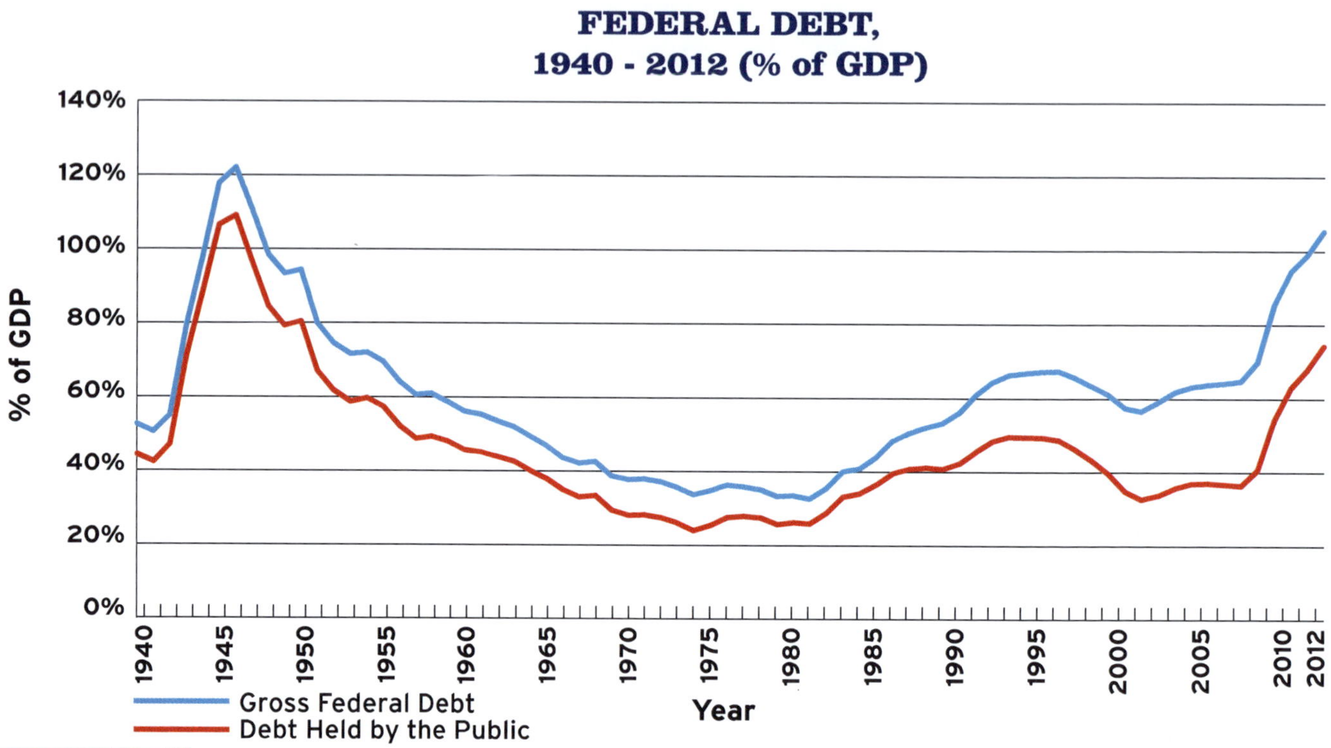

FIGURE 4 SOURCE: Budget of the U.S. Government FY 2013, http://www.gpo.gov/fdsys/pkg/BUDGET-2013-TAB/xls/BUDGET-2013-TAB-7-1.xls.

DEBT IN THE OBAMA ADMINISTRATION

When President Obama was sworn into office on January 20, 2009, the U.S. had a total of $10.6 trillion in debt outstanding, according to the Treasury Department's Bureau of the Public Debt. For the reasons described above, the debt has increased precipitously since then. In fact, as of September 30, 2013, the U.S. government had a total of $12.0 trillion in debt held by the public and $4.76 trillion in intra-governmental holdings, for a total of $16.7 trillion in outstanding debt. This represents a 58 percent increase in gross debt in less than five years.

From one perspective, the U.S. has accrued too much debt. At the end of FY 2013, gross federal debt had reached 100 percent of GDP, up from just 69.7 percent at the end of FY 2008. However, some argue that gross debt, which combines debt held by the public and intra-governmental holdings, is not the proper measure to use when calculating the ratio of debt to GDP. Instead, these critics claim that net debt—in other words, only the debt held by the public, and not debt created through intra-governmental transfers—should be used in these calculations. Using this latter method, the debt-to-GDP ratio at the end of FY 2013 was 71.9 percent, and the ratio was expected to fall to around more than 71 percent by the end of FY 2023. In these terms, the growth of federal debt appears much less threatening.

The debt has grown so quickly because of large and repeated annual deficits in federal spending. In FY 2009, the fiscal year in which the recent economic crisis was at its worst and in which the federal government spent over $1 trillion in stimulus funding, the deficit was $1.41 trillion, the result of $3.52 trillion in outlays and only $2.11 trillion in receipts. Deficits in FY 2012 and FY 2013 were $1.09 trillion and $680 billion, respectively.

Such large sums are difficult to conceptualize properly. To put the situation in perspective, if the federal government spent its yearly revenues exclusively on debt reduction and ceased all of its operations, it would take three or four years to pay down all the debt. Or, the government could pay down the debt in one blow if it simply took more than $52,000 from every person living in the U.S., including children, the elderly, and the unemployed. If this one-time "debt reduction fee" were levied only on those in the workforce, the cost would be over $106,000 per person.

From another perspective, cutting spending on commonly targeted programs is unlikely to resolve the problem. Deficit hawks often call for cuts to what they describe as unnecessary federal programs like the National Endowment for the Arts. However, the NEA's bill is actually quite small. At today's funding levels, the Endowment could operate for more than 100,000 years before it ran up a bill as large as the current federal debt.

THE BENEFITS OF DEBT

Though current levels of federal spending may seem alarming, with trillion-dollar deficits and rapidly rising gross debt, it is important to remember that federal debt serves a valid purpose in ensuring a functional government. Alexander Hamilton famously recognized this when serving as the first U.S. Secretary of the Treasury. In 1781, when the young country was facing the challenge of repaying debts created during the Revolutionary War, Hamilton wrote, "A national debt, if it is not excessive, will be to us a national blessing." He argued that by incurring and then paying off debts a country could build a reputation as a safe haven for investors. This faith would then allow the government to raise large amounts of money very quickly in times of need, such as wars or economic crises, through the sale of government bonds.

Similarly, some economists today believe that government spending in a time of economic recession is a good thing, even when it leads to significant increases in debt and deficit. Paul Krugman, one of the most adamant proponents of this Keynesian economic doctrine, has argued that the ballooning of government deficit and debt is not yet a reason to worry. By stimulating demand through increased spending, Krugman has argued, the government can stimulate economic growth. This will set the nation back on the path of economic growth, allowing the government to repay the debts it had incurred.

WHAT NOW?

Given today's fiscal circumstances, how should the government deal with its debt and its annual balance of receipts and outlays?

Members of the Republican Party, especially those who have aligned themselves with the Tea Party, believe that the government should severely curtail its spending. A common cry among these groups is that "the government has a spending problem, not a revenue problem." It is this fiscal ideology that led to sequestration, the deep across-the-board cuts that went into effect on March 1, 2013. These policies are also reflected in the fiscally conservative House budget, which was drafted in large part by Representative Paul Ryan (R-Wisc.), chairman of the House Budget Committee. It is interesting to note that these plans generally call for substantial cuts in spending but do not raise taxes, which would also reduce the federal debt.

On the other hand, many politicians and economists argue that drastic reductions in federal spending would be harmful at this time, when the economy is still recovering. They claim that federal spending is needed to spur the economic growth that will lead the country out of recession. As evidence, they point to European countries, like Greece, that have enacted austerity measures. Although government outlays have decreased sharply in these countries, economic indicators such as unemployment rates show that their economies continue to struggle. According to the opponents of fiscal conservatives, this demonstrates that cuts in federal spending will not solve the problem.

Even once the decision has been made to cut spending or to raise taxes, though, specific choices will remain difficult.

What programs should be cut? Republicans often suggest cuts to Head Start, Medicaid, and other "social safety net" programs; Democrats argue that these cuts would unfairly harm those in most need of assistance. On the other hand, Democrats regularly call for cuts in spending on defense and homeland security; Republicans counter that these cuts would result in a country vulnerable to attacks.

What taxes should be raised? An increase in the corporate tax rate could quickly raise billions, but fiscal conservatives argue that this would hurt American businesses and encourage companies to move their jobs overseas. By restoring the individual income tax to its pre-Bush levels, the government could take a substantial chunk out of its debts, but American families would have thousands less to spend every year as a consequence. Alternatively, the government could also levy a new tax, such as a tax on carbon emissions, or increase taxes that are currently low by global standards, such as the federal gasoline tax. But, this would reduce consumption and restrict some productive activities.

The problem is stark, but the answers are far from clear. This project, the Annual Report of the U.S.A., aims to clarify the issues by providing information on federal revenues and outlays that will help American citizens make informed judgments with respect to the federal budget.

★

AMERICA'S FINANCES: NET INTEREST

by Daniel Backman

Just as most people borrow money from a bank when buying a house or a car, the federal government borrows money to pay for the expenditures that it does not fully fund at the time of purchase. In both cases, while paying the lender back, the borrower (either the home buyer or the government) also pays the lender some percentage of the original loan in interest. This interest compensates the lender for the service of providing cash when needed, and it also remunerates the lender for parting with money that he or she could have invested elsewhere (this is called the opportunity cost). In addition, interest rewards the lender for taking the risk that the borrower may not pay back the loan amount in full.

The U.S. government lends and borrows trillions of dollars every year, and it either pays or collects interest on most of these loans. To borrow money, the Department of the Treasury issues Treasury securities: Treasury bills, Treasury bonds, Treasury notes, and Treasury Inflation-Protected Securities (TIPS). Treasuries, as such securities are often called, represent a loan from the buyer to the U.S. government. The period of time between purchase of a Treasury and repayment, known as the security's maturity, ranges from one month to 30 years.[1]

The U.S. government also receives interest payments on loans and investments it makes. For example, the federal government earned an estimated $1.3 billion in interest on loans made to states to help fund their unemployment benefit programs during FY 2012.[2]

Together, the interest paid on Treasury securities and the returns made on loans and investments comprise the net interest component of the federal budget. For at least 70 years, the government has paid more in interest than it has received.[3]

Treasuries are used to finance both the government's annual budget deficits and the federal debt. Consequently, it is not possible to talk about net interest without talking about the national debt.

NET INTEREST AND THE NATIONAL DEBT: A BRIEF HISTORY

Since its earliest days, the United States has financed its government operations in part by issuing debt. In 1776, the Continental Army funded its fight against the British by borrowing from France and the Netherlands. In 1789, Alexander Hamilton, the first Secretary of the Treasury, wrote that "a national debt, if not excessive, will be to us a national blessing."[4] Indeed, with the singular exception of a few months after January 1835, the United States has owed interest on debt for its entire history as a nation.[5]

Historical records demonstrate the relationship between the national debt and net interest, which is largely made up of the interest paid on that debt. Figure 5 shows both publicly held debt and net interest owed as a percent of GDP.[6]

1 "Federal Debt and Interest Costs," Congressional Budget Office, December 2010: 6.
2 "Analytical Perspectives, Budget of the United States Government, Fiscal Year 2014," Office of Management and Budget, February 13, 2012: Table 32-1.
3 "Fiscal Year 2014 Historical Tables," Office of Management and Budget, 2013.
4 "The 18th Century," Bureau of the Public Debt, http://www.publicdebt.treas.gov/history/1700.htm.
5 "The 19th Century," Bureau of the Public Debt, http://www.publicdebt.treas.gov/history/1800.htm.
6 "Fiscal Year 2012 Historical Tables," Office of Management and Budget, 2011.

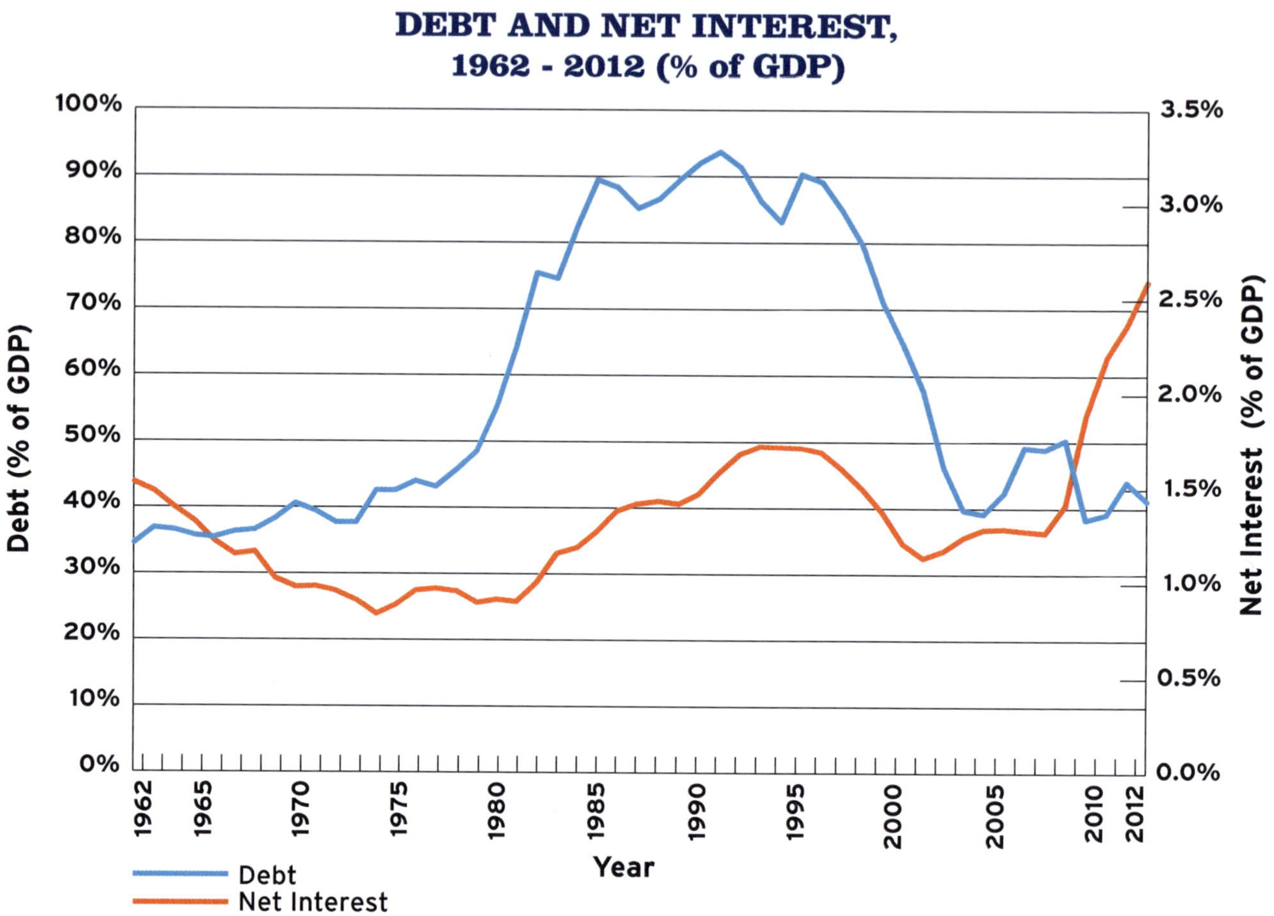

FIGURE 5 SOURCE: Budget of the U.S. Government FY 2013, http://www.gpo.gov/fdsys/pkg/BUDGET-2013-TAB/xls/BUDGET-2013-TAB-3-2.xls and http://www.gpo.gov/fdsys/pkg/BUDGET-2013-TAB/xls/BUDGET-2013-TAB-7-1.xls.

As this graph shows, there is generally a positive relationship between the size of the national debt and the size of net interest payments. Generally, the more the federal government owes, the more interest it must pay to its lenders. Yet, as this figure also makes clear, the relationship fluctuates.

WHAT DETERMINES NET INTEREST: DEBT, RISK, INFLATION, AND THE MARKET FOR TREASURIES

Size of Debt and Associated Default Risk

When the federal government borrows more money, not only does it pay additional interest because it has taken out a bigger loan, it often has to borrow at a higher interest rate. That occurs because, as discussed above, the interest rate rewards lenders both for parting with their money and for risking default (in other words, the chance that the borrower will fail to pay back the loan). A potential lender who sees the government increasing its debt may begin to doubt the government's ability to pay the money back. The government must then offer a higher interest rate to get the lender to make the loan. And while the U.S. government is one of the most reliable borrowers in the world, default risk is always present to some degree.

In fact, default risk plays a role in loans throughout the economy. For example, imagine that a man named Greg wants to buy a car, but, like most people, he doesn't have enough money sitting around to pay for the car in cash. So, he applies for a 5-year, $30,000 loan from the local bank. The bank examines his credit, including his income and how much other debt he has, and grants him a loan at 3.0 percent interest compounded annually.

The next day, after impressing his wife with his new ride, Greg decides to buy her a car as well. He goes back to the local bank and applies for another $30,000 loan. But this time, the bank sees that he already has $30,000 in debt, plus interest, and knows there is a greater risk that he won't be able to pay back two loans than just one. This time, the bank grants him a second loan at 4.0 percent annual interest. The increase in interest rate is meant to account for the added risk.

TABLE 1 - SCENARIO: GREG'S CAR LOANS

	Interest Rate	Initial Loan Amount (Principal)	Interest Owed After 1 Year*	Interest Owed After 5 Years
Car #1	3%	$30,000.00	$900.00	$4,778.22
Car #2	4%	$30,000.00	$1,200.00	$6,499.59
Total		**$60,000.00**	**$2,100.00**	**$11,277.81**

As the above table demonstrates, although Greg doubled his debt by buying a second car, he more than doubled the amount he owed in interest due to the higher interest rate on the second loan.

Inflation and the Market for Treasury Securities

In addition to the amount of outstanding government debt and the associated default risk, two other factors help determine the net interest owed by the federal government: the supply and demand for Treasury securities, and inflation.

The supply of Treasuries depends on how much money the government needs to borrow. The more money the government needs, the more it is willing to pay in interest to encourage investors to lend.

On the other hand, the demand for Treasuries depends on how many people want to buy U.S. debt and where else they could invest their money. When a lot of people want to buy Treasuries, which are seen as very low-risk investments, the government can offer a lower interest rate to borrow the money it needs. Conversely, if interest rates on other investments are attractively high and those investments are not seen as being too risky, the government must offer even higher interest rates to incentivize lenders to buy its debt instead of putting their money elsewhere.

A fourth factor, inflation, also has an effect on interest rates for Treasuries. Inflation is a measure of how much prices are increasing in an economy. For example, if inflation is 2 percent, prices will be 2 percent higher in a year than they are now; in other words, a dollar today can only buy about 98 cents worth of goods a year from now.[7] Thus, a lender would have to charge 2 percent interest just to have the same purchasing power in a year that he has today.

7 Using the present value formula: 1.00/(1+0.02)^1 = 0.9804.

The other determinants of interest rates, such as opportunity cost and default risk, are generally added on top of the inflation rate. This total rate is called the nominal interest rate. The interest rate minus the rate of inflation is called the real interest rate.

NET INTEREST TODAY AND IN THE NEAR FUTURE

In FY 2013, net interest accounted for approximately $259 billion in federal spending.[8] At about 1.5 percent of GDP, that amount is on the lower side by recent historical standards.[9] That is because, despite the large national debt, interest rates in recent years have been extremely low. As interest rates rise to more typical levels, however, net interest is projected to more than double as a share of GDP, from 1.5 percent in 2014 to 2.2 percent in 2024.[10]

PROJECTED NET INTEREST AND PUBLIC DEBT, 2012 - 2023 (% of GDP)

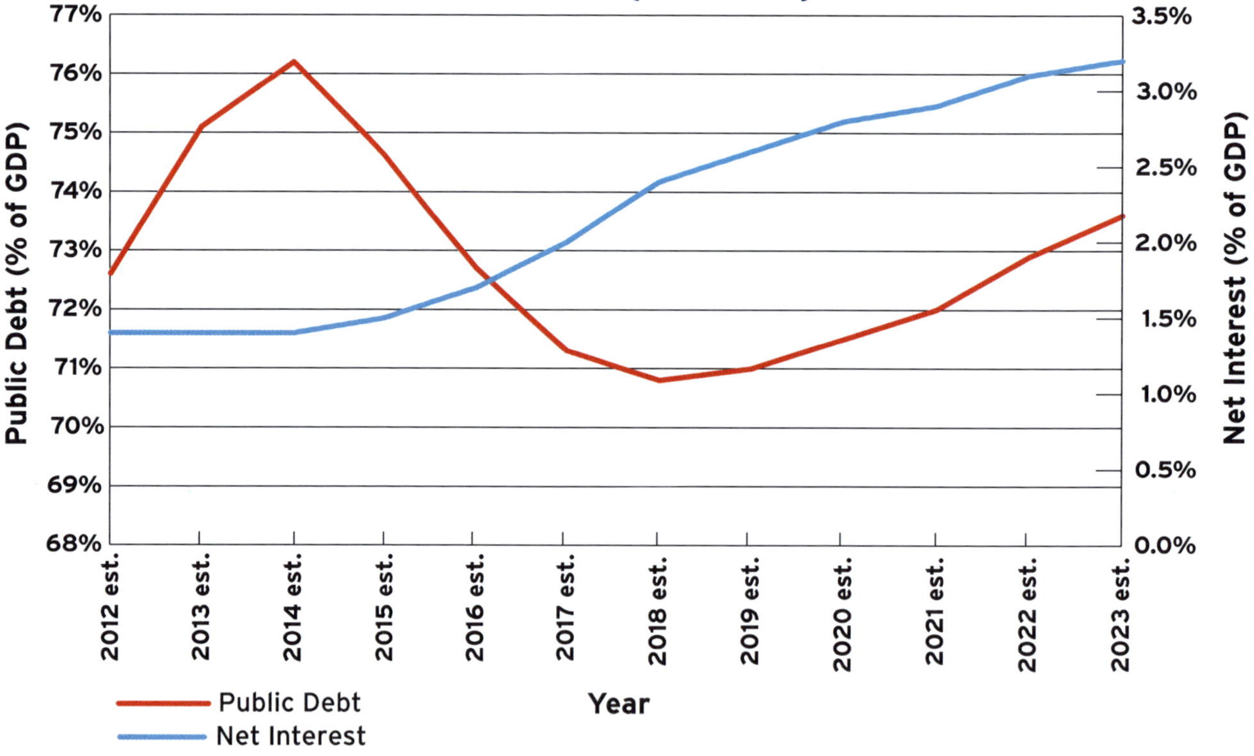

FIGURE 6 SOURCE: Congressional Budget Office, http://www.cbo.gov/sites/default/files/cbofiles/attachments/March2012Baseline.pdf.

Figure 6 illustrates the effect low interest rates have had on net interest.[11] While the debt grew from about 36.0 percent of GDP in 2007 to 73.2 percent of GDP in 2012, net interest as a percentage of GDP actually fell from 1.7 percent to 1.4 percent in that same period. As interest rates rise in the coming years, the national debt is projected to fall from a peak of 76.2 percent of GDP in 2014 to 70.8 percent in 2018 due to budget cuts and a healthier economy. Yet, over that same period, net interest is projected to increase from 1.4 percent of GDP to 2.4 percent.

8 "Analytical Perspectives."
9 "The Budget and Economic Outlook: Fiscal Years 2013-2023," Congressional Budget Office, February 2013.
10 "The Budget and Economic Outlook," 25.
11 Data from "Historical Tables" (2007-2010) and "Updated Budget Projections: Fiscal Years 2012 to 2022", Congressional Budget Office, March 2012, (2012-2022).

WHY INTEREST RATES ARE SO LOW

Interest rates on Treasury securities today are at historic lows. In 2012, the nominal interest rate on a 3-month Treasury bill was 0.09 percent. Moreover, interest rates throughout the 2000s have been markedly low by historical standards. Figure 7 shows interest rates on 3-month T-bills from January 1934 to December 2012.[12]

INTEREST RATE ON A 3-MONTH TREASURY BILL, 1934 - 2012

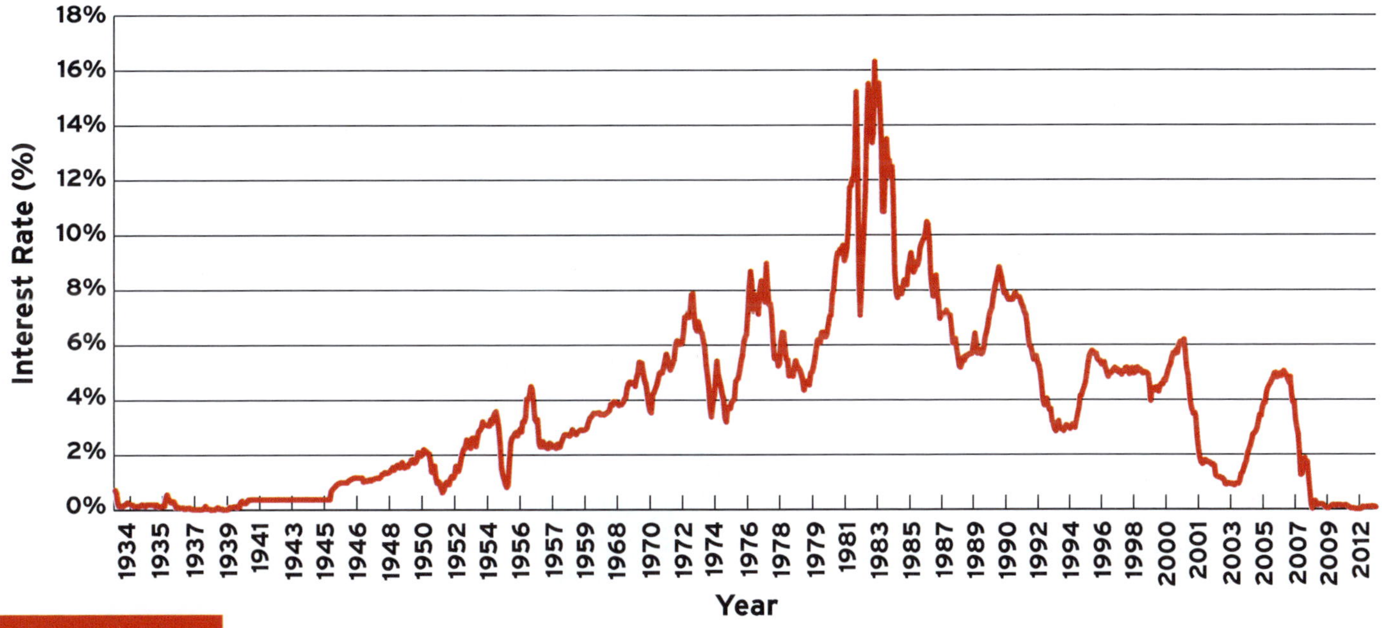

FIGURE 7 SOURCE: Federal Reserve Economic Data, http://research.stlouisfed.org/fred2/series/TB3MS.

As the graph indicates, and as is the case with other maturities as well as many bonds throughout the economy, interest rates on 3-month T-bills are at levels not seen since the Great Depression. Several explanations for these low rates relate to the economic conditions of a severe, protracted recession.

For one, the Federal Reserve will often act to lower market interest rates when the economy is contracting. The Fed's expansionary monetary policy involves, among other actions, buying short-term Treasury bills. With fewer bills remaining on the market, demand increases and the interest rate decreases as a result. The most recent recession saw enormous expansionary efforts by the Fed.[13]

In addition, recessions often come with periods of low inflation, known as disinflation. When consumers want to buy fewer goods than usual, the price of these goods does not increase as quickly. Inflation rates in the 2007-2009 recession were low and, at times, negative (called "deflation").[14] The last major period of disinflation and deflation was, as one might guess, the Great Depression. As discussed above, lower inflation is associated with lower nominal interest rates.

12 Data from the "Federal Reserve Economic Data," Federal Reserve Bank of St. Louis, http://research.stlouisfed.org/fred2/.
13 To learn more about the Federal Reserve's monetary policy tools, see http://www.frbsf.org/publications/federalreserve/fedinbrief/guides.html.
14 "Consumer Price Index," Bureau of Labor Statistics, 2012, http://www.bls.gov/cpi/.

Finally, since U.S. Treasuries are perceived as a virtually risk-free asset, investors often rush to buy Treasuries when investing elsewhere seems too risky. Times of high risk, including recessions, tend to increase the demand for Treasuries and further lower the interest rate. In the 2008 global financial crisis, not only Americans but also investors worldwide flocked to U.S. Treasuries to keep their money safe from rampant risk across the globe. Europe's subsequent sovereign debt crisis only exacerbated this trend.

WHEN INTEREST RATES REMAIN LOW

What has generated greater debate, however, is the extended period of low interest rates in the early 2000s. After the recession of 2001-2002, the economy began growing again, but interest rates, which traditionally follow growth, remained low. Two competing theories seek to explain this phenomenon.

One, put forth by Stanford economist John Taylor, claims that the Federal Reserve intentionally kept interest rates abnormally low in order to feed economic growth. According to Taylor, given the levels of unemployment and inflation, the Fed should have targeted higher interest rates during much of this period.[15]

> **"The unusually low interest rate decisions were, of course, made with careful consideration by monetary policy makers. One can interpret them as purposeful deviations from the 'regular' interest rate settings based on the usual macroeconomic variables." — John Taylor**

Alternatively, the current chairman of the Federal Reserve, Ben Bernanke, attributed lower interest rates on many global assets, including U.S. Treasury securities, to excessive global saving that increased the supply of loanable funds and lowered interest rates on these assets. In 2005, Bernanke postulated the existence of a "global saving glut" that led to high savers in developing countries purchasing assets in industrialized nations like the United States, thereby dampening interest rates.[16]

> **"[O]ver the past decade a combination of diverse forces has created a significant increase in the global supply of saving—a global saving glut—which helps to explain...the relatively low level of long-term real interest rates in the world today." — Ben Bernanke**

NET INTEREST AND THE SPECTER OF DEFAULT

Still, economists and policymakers generally agree that recent low interest rates should not be taken as a sign that the national debt can continue to grow indefinitely. As previously noted, the CBO expects interest rates to increase as the economy recovers. Further, depending on the policy choices Congress and the President make, investors may begin to perceive increased default risk on Treasuries and demand higher rates.

To gain a better understanding of default risk, recall the above story about Greg and the car loans. The interest Greg owed more than doubled when he doubled the amount he borrowed. As shown in Table 1, Greg's total indebtedness after five years also more than doubled with the purchase of an second car, from $34,800 to $71,300.

15 John B. Taylor, "The Financial Crisis and the Policy Responses: An Empirical Analysis of What Went Wrong," A Festschrift in Honor of David Dodge, Bank of Canada, November 2008.

16 Ben S. Bernanke, "The Global Saving Glut and the U.S. Current Account Deficit," Virginia Association of Economists, Richmond, VA, April 14, 2005.

If Greg tried to get a third loan, banks would respond to his additional debt load by charging an even higher interest rate. This cycle of increased debt leading to increased interest rates and increased debts through interest payments would make the likelihood of Greg defaulting ever greater.

Some economists and policymakers fear a similarly inexorable fate for the U.S. federal government. This has already happened to some extent in Europe. Large debt buildups in Greece and other countries on the Euro common currency have led to increased borrowing costs. These costs have in turn raised the specter of default and further fueled the rise in interest rates.

As macroeconomist and Harvard Kennedy School professor Jeffrey Frankel said, "The arithmetic of the interest payments can turn an apparently sustainable fiscal situation into an explosive path very quickly. This is extremely hard to reverse once it happens." Frankel argued that the best way for governments to avoid this fate is to cut deficits in years of healthy economic growth to compensate for deficits amassed in recessionary years.

"The only solution is to take the opportunity of the upswing of the business cycle to run strong budgets, preferably surpluses. This is what the U.S. did in the late 1990s," explained Frankel. "But the U.S., along with the U.K. and [the Euro zone] forgot this basic principle during the years 2003 to 2007. Now we are all beginning to pay the price."[17]

Two other economists, Carmen Reinhart of the University of Maryland and Kenneth Rogoff of Harvard University, studied eight centuries of sovereign debt and financial crises to further inform the debate. "Those who would point to low servicing costs should remember that market interest rates can change like the weather," they concluded. "Debt levels, by contrast, can't be brought down quickly. Even though politicians everywhere like to argue that their country will expand its way out of debt, our historical research suggests that growth alone is rarely enough to achieve that with the debt levels we are experiencing today."[18]

Still, Princeton economist Paul Krugman has maintained that U.S. politicians should presently focus on growing the economy rather than shrinking the deficit. In reference to the Euro crisis, he wrote that "what Greek experience actually shows is that while running deficits in good times can get you in trouble… Trying to eliminate deficits once you're already in trouble is a recipe for depression."[19]

Further, Krugman has argued that the cycle described above, in which rising debt leads to a higher perceived risk of default and, consequently, even higher interest costs, is not inevitable. To support this claim, Krugman noted that Britain and the U.S. pay lenders at an interest rate of 2 percent, while Japan, which is even more indebted than Greece, pays only 1 percent interest.[20]

★

17 Jeffrey Frankel, e-mail message to author, June 11, 2012.

18 Carmen Reinhart and Kenneth Rogoff, "Too Much Debt Means the Economy Can't Grow: Reinhart and Rogoff," Bloomberg, July 13, 2011, http://www.bloombergview.com/articles/2011-07-14/too-much-debt-means-economy-can-t-grow-commentary-by-reinhart-and-rogoff.

19 Paul Krugman, "What Greece Means," *New York Times*, March 11, 2011, http://www.nytimes.com/2012/03/12/opinion/krugman-what-greece-means.html.

20 Paul Krugman, "What Ails Europe?" *New York Times*, February 26, 2012, http://www.nytimes.com/2012/02/27/opinion/krugman-what-ails-europe.html.

AMERICA'S FINANCES: TAXES

by Ross Svenson

Americans began the year 2013 facing a massive tax increase. If Congress had allowed the country to jump off the "fiscal cliff" of simultaneous tax increases and spending reductions, Americans' tax rates on average would have increased five percentage points in 2013, according to the Tax Policy Center.[21] Through a patchwork of last-minute fixes in the waning hours of 2012, however, Congress kept the average tax rate increase to less than two percentage points. While Congress temporarily stayed the fiscal blow, they did not solve the underlying problems of inequity and inefficiency in the federal tax code. Nor did Congress find a way to make the tax code an asset in lowering annual deficits or the national debt.

Democrats and Republicans both agree that the system urgently needs reform as these issues of inequity, inefficiency, and growing debt have reached a tipping point. Serious bipartisan tax reform proposals indeed abound, ranging from the Simpson-Bowles Commission report to the Domenici-Rivlin plan. These proposals offer a simpler tax code that eliminates costly tax expenditures and lowers rates. These frameworks provide hope for reducing our growing federal debt. Real ideological differences, as well as partisan posturing, however, will likely impede meaningful change.

The Problem with Tax Expenditures

TOP INDIVIDUAL & CORPORATE TAX RATES, 1909 - 2013

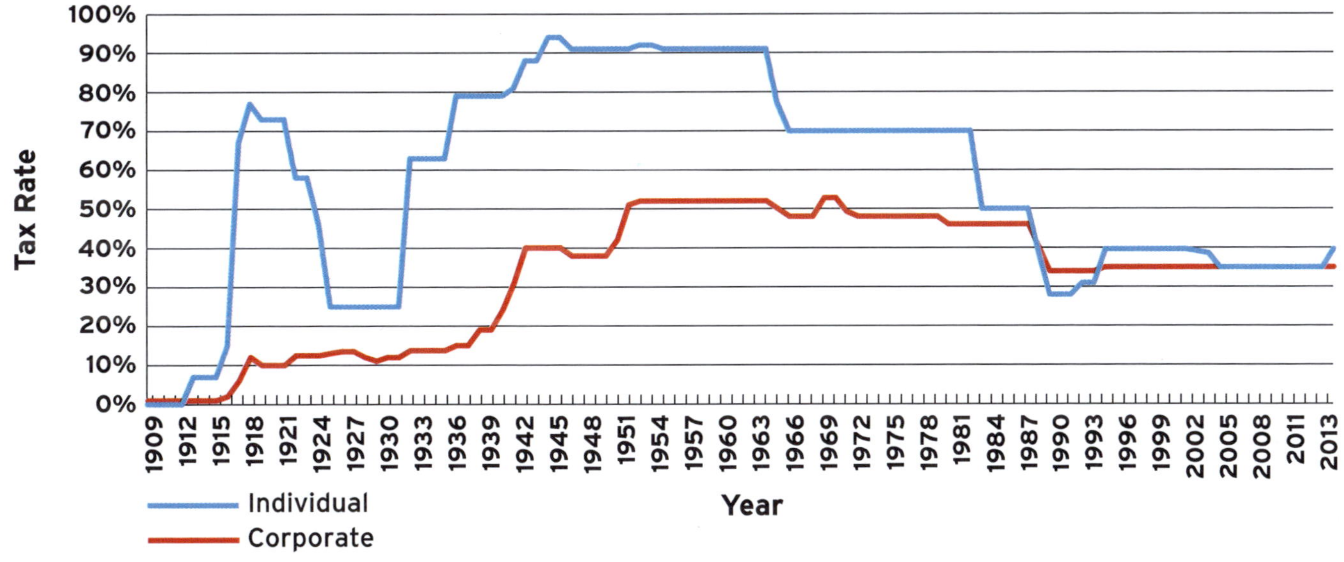

FIGURE 8

SOURCE: Tax Policy Center and Tax Foundation: http://www.taxpolicycenter.org/taxfacts/Content/PDF/corporate_historical_bracket.pdf, http://taxfoundation.org/article/us-federal-individual-income-tax-rates-history-1913-2013-nominal-and-inflation-adjusted-brackets.

The fiscal cliff deal, or the 2013 American Tax Relief Act, accomplished some good. It reinstated a level of certainty for American taxpayers by settling the question of the Bush tax cuts. The law permanently extended the 2001 and 2003 Bush tax cuts for individuals earning under $400,000 per year and couples earning under

21 Howard Gleckman, "The Fiscal Cliff Deal in One Picture," *Forbes*, January 10, 2013, http://www.forbes.com/sites/beltway/2013/01/10/the-fiscal-cliff-deal-in-one-picture/.

$450,000 per year and eliminated the tax cuts for those earning more.[22] The law also permanently capped itemized deductions for individuals making over $250,000 per year and couples making over $300,000 per year, increased the estate tax from 35 percent to 40 percent for estates over $5 million, and tied the alternative minimum tax to inflation. The corporate tax rate remained set at 35 percent. These tax issues had been hanging over the heads of taxpayers for the last decade, and Congress had previously only offered temporary extensions and delays. Further, from a historical perspective, the top individual and corporate tax rates remain historically low despite the slight uptick in the top individual income tax.

Yet, the compromise did little to fix America's "messy" tax code. In a 2012 document released by the U.S. Government Accountability Office, the U.S. Treasury Department reported 173 "tax expenditures," or government spending through the tax code, for FY 2011, totaling $1 trillion.[23] These expenditures in the form of tax credits, deductions, and exclusions come at a steep cost to the federal government at a time when the federal debt stands at over $16 trillion.

In the latter portion of the 2012 presidential election, much attention centered on Mitt Romney's comments regarding the 47 percent of Americans who did not pay federal income taxes. Looked at one way, 47 percent of Americans paid no federal income taxes in 2010 because a variety of tax expenditures supported by both Democrats and Republicans zeroed out federal income taxes for many middle and lower income individuals.[24] However, most of these Americans still paid payroll taxes, even as they offset their income taxes with these popular tax breaks. For example, the poor can qualify for the Earned Income Tax Credit. For all Americans, employer-sponsored health insurance is excluded from taxable income; likewise pension contributions are tax-exempt for all. Workers can deduct their mortgage interest payments and charitable giving. If individuals have children, they receive a child tax credit. These tax breaks make up a large portion of tax expenditures.

INDIVIDUAL INCOME TAX EXPENDITURES, 2013

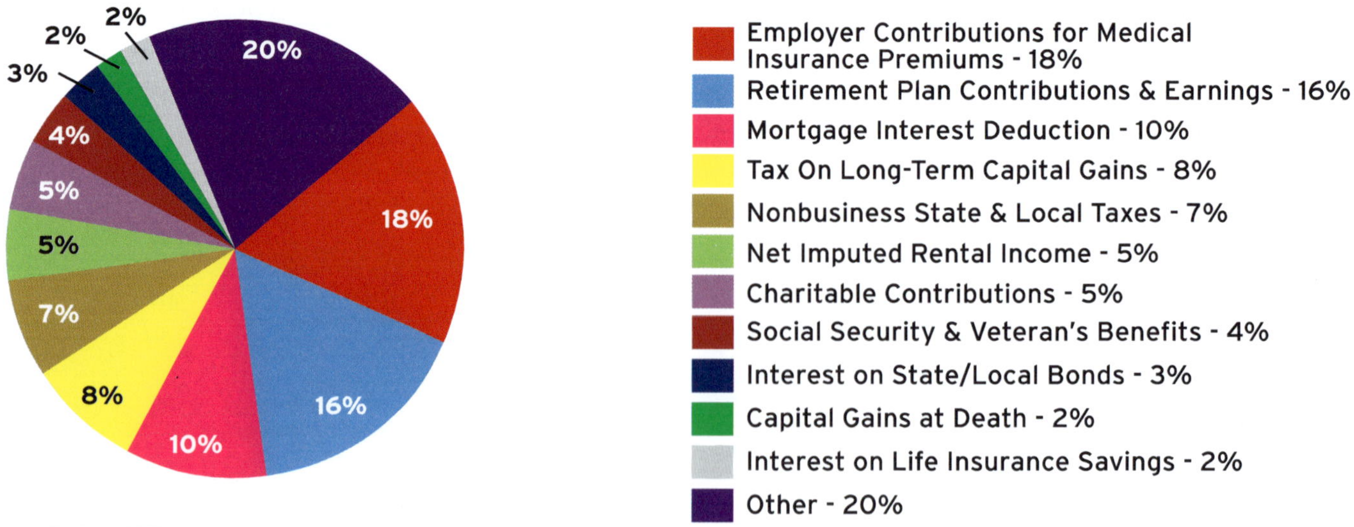

FIGURE 9

SOURCE: Internal Revenue Service.
http://www.taxpayeradvocate.irs.gov/userfiles/file/Full-Report/Volume-1.pdf.

22 Matt Smith, "Obama Signs Bill Warding Off Fiscal Cliff," CNN, January 3, 2013, http://www.cnn.com/2013/01/02/politics/fiscal-cliff/index.html.
23 "Tax Expenditures: Background and Evaluation Criteria and Questions," U.S. Government Accountability Office, November 29, 2012, http://www.gao.gov/assets/660/650371.pdf.
24 "Who Doesn't Pay Federal Taxes?," Tax Policy Center, http://www.taxpolicycenter.org/taxtopics/federal-taxes-households.cfm.

While the poor and middle class benefit from these tax expenditures, however, wealthy Americans do so comparatively more. According to the Congressional Budget Office, more than half of the combined benefits of those tax expenditures (the ten largest tax expenditures) accrued to households with income in the highest quintile of the population in 2013.[25]

COST OF MAJOR TAX EXPENDITURES BY INCOME GROUP, 2013

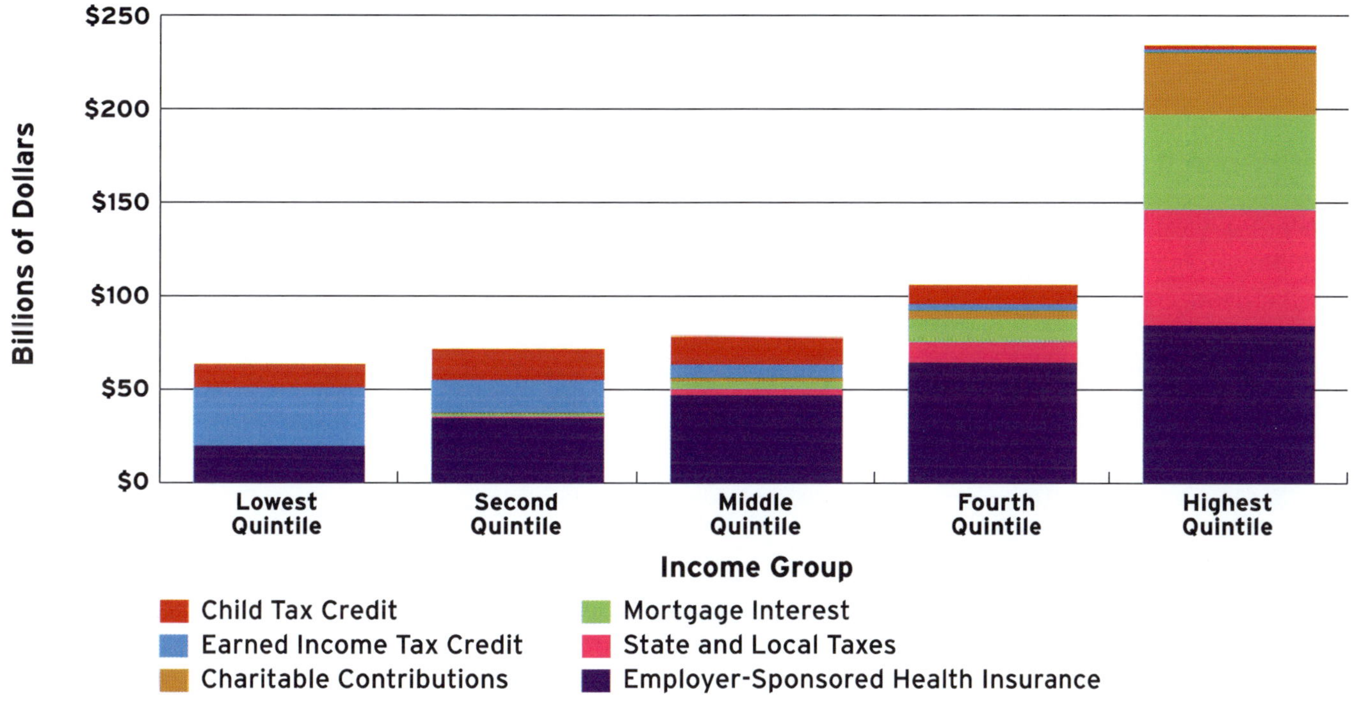

FIGURE 10 SOURCE: Congressional Budget Office, http://www.cbo.gov/sites/default/files/cbofiles/attachments/43768-SuppData.xls.

Similarly, between the years 2008 and 2010, a report published by Citizens for Tax Justice and the Institute on Taxation and Economic Policy documented that 30 major U.S. corporations paid no federal income taxes.[26] These companies successfully avoided paying income taxes by benefiting from a number of tax breaks and loopholes. Companies can deduct the declining value of equipment and machinery faster than it actually depreciates; they can deduct executive stock options; they can earn research and development tax credits; and they can defer taxation of income earned abroad through foreign subsidiaries.

Michael Linden, managing director for economic policy at the Center for American Progress, noted that while many tax breaks, particularly the largest tax expenditures such as the exclusion of employer-provided health care benefits and the mortgage interest deduction, serve "legitimate public interests," that does not mean "the current way we do it is the best way, and it doesn't mean they can't be reduced somewhat."[27]

25 "The Distribution of Major Tax Expenditures in the Individual Income Tax System," Congressional Budget Office, May 29, 2013, http://www.cbo.gov/publication/43768.
26 Kevin Drawbaugh, "Thirty Companies Paid No U.S. Income Tax 2008-2010: Report," *Reuters*, November 3, 2011, http://www.reuters.com/article/2011/11/03/us-usa-tax-corporate-idUSTRE7A261C20111103.
27 Michael Linden, interview by author, September 24, 2013.

Many of these tax expenditures, as noted by the Congressional Budget Office, disproportionately benefit high income-earners. Linden explained, "The value to the taxpayer is dependent on their tax rate." In other words, he said, "If you're in the top tax bracket, a dollar excluded from your income because of [the employer-sponsored insurance exclusion] is worth almost 40 cents to you, but if you're in the 20 percent tax bracket, it's only worth 20 cents to you." The Tax Policy Center notes that taxpayers at the bottom of income distribution can only reap benefits from refundable tax credits, yet 81 percent of tax expenditures are deductions or exclusions.

The complicated code also creates inefficiency. According to Senate Finance Committee reports, 59 percent of taxpayers hire preparers to file their taxes for them, while another 30 percent use tax preparation software. This outside assistance is necessary for most people as the tax code has grown 33,454 pages since 1995. Confusion over the tax code results in a "tax gap"—the difference owed in taxes between that which is paid—of $385 billion and "an underpayment of approximately 14 percent of the estimated tax liability." The tax breaks can create inefficiencies in a larger sense, too, by distorting the market. For instance, as Linden noted, many homeowners purchase more expensive homes than they normally would because they anticipate the mortgage interest deduction.

NUMBER OF PAGES IN FEDERAL TAX CODE, 1913 - 2013

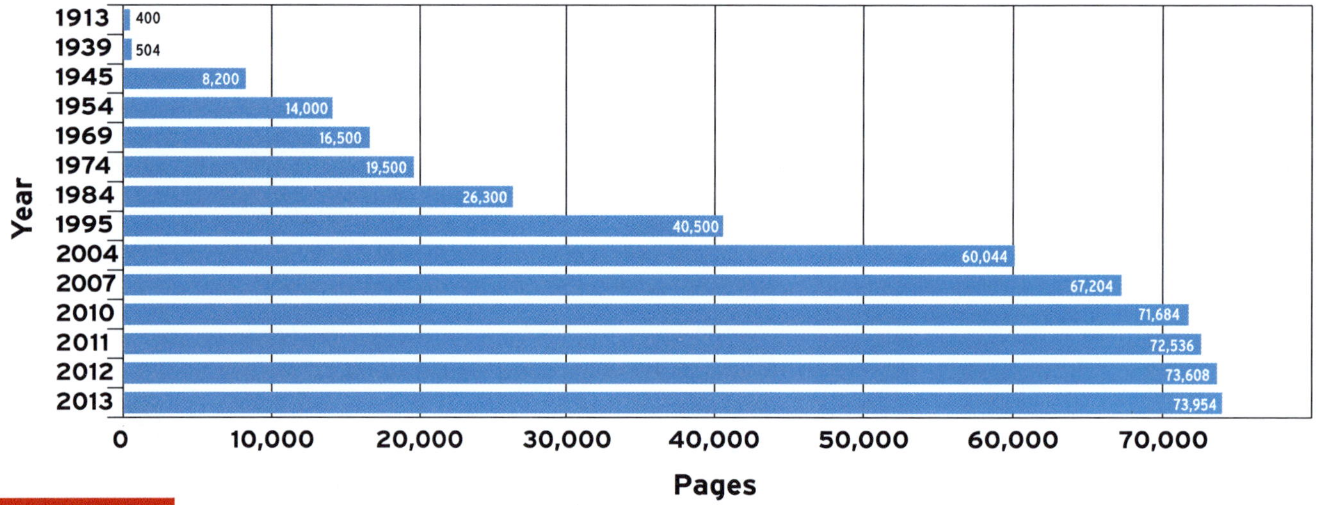

FIGURE 11 SOURCE: Congressional Budget Office, http://www.cbo.gov/sites/default/files/cbofiles/attachments/43768-SuppData.xls.

Bipartisan Action Plans: Simpson-Bowles and Domenici-Rivlin

Most tax reform plans in vogue today were born out of commissions and working groups tasked with identifying ways to shrink the growth rate of the national debt. With this goal in mind, most tax reform plans seek to cut costly tax expenditures, simplify the overall code, and ultimately generate more revenue. Most plans also seek to maintain progressivity and improve efficiency. The Simpson-Bowles Plan, produced by former Senator Alan Simpson (R-Wyo.) and former Clinton Chief of Staff Erskine Bowles as chairs of the President's Fiscal Commission in December 2010, would accomplish these goals, albeit with some politically unpopular provisions. The plan lowers overall federal income tax rates substantially by eliminating all but a few tax expenditures.[28]

28 "Moment of Truth," National Commission on Fiscal Responsibility and Reform, December 2010, http://www.fiscalcommission.gov/sites/fiscalcommission.gov/files/documents/TheMomentofTruth12_1_2010.pdf.

Why keep any tax expenditures? As observed earlier, tax expenditures, properly constructed, serve legitimate public interests. The Simpson-Bowles Plan maintains tax expenditures that "promote work, home ownership, health care, charity, and savings"—all of which have positive effects on the economy as a whole. The plan would make alterations, however, to the tax breaks that promote these objectives in the current system. For example, the mortgage interest deduction that is currently capped at $1 million for principal and second residences would become a 12 percent non-refundable tax credit with a qualifying mortgage capped at $500,000 and no credit for interest from a second residence. This change limits the cost of the tax expenditure, saving money, and makes the break more beneficial for low-income earners. The tax break is worth the same amount for all income brackets.

From the corporate angle, the plan makes efficiency and a sound business environment its goals. The corporate tax rate would be sharply reduced from 35 percent to between 23 and 29 percent. To do so, all corporate tax expenditures are eliminated. Finally, the Simpson-Bowles Plan advocates for a territorial tax system, which would exempt profits made overseas permanently from domestic taxation. Under the current tax code, these profits are immune from taxation as long as they are not repatriated. Thus, companies seldom repatriate foreign profits. Since we do not gather much revenue from the current system anyway, advocates of the territorial tax system say we might as well encourage the repatriation of this corporate income to generate economic growth domestically.

Another plan that seeks to tackle the federal tax code on its way to deficit reduction is the Bipartisan Policy Center's Plan crafted by former Director of the Office of Management and Budget Alice Rivlin and former Senator Pete Domenici (R-N. Mex). They also look to eliminate most tax expenditures and alter the few they keep. The most significant difference between the Simpson-Bowles Plan and the Domenici-Rivlin Plan is the presence of a so-called "Deficit Reduction Sales Tax" in the latter.[29] This tax would operate akin to a Value-Added Tax, which exists in many countries. Businesses would "pay tax on all their sales, but receive credits for taxes that their suppliers pay when they purchase materials and capital goods from other firms." While perhaps adding a layer of complexity to the tax code, it would accomplish the goal of combating the growth in the federal debt.

A Legislative Path Forward?

Representative Dave Camp (R-Mich.), House Ways and Means Committee Chairman, and Senator Max Baucus (D-Mont.), Senate Finance Committee Chairman, have publicly made crafting a tax reform plan their mission in the 113th Congress. The pair made stops across the country this summer to promote tax reform, according to a *Politico* article highlighting their efforts.[30] While they seek a bipartisan compromise, most agree it can not be achieved in the present political climate.

For one, President Obama has not put his political muscle behind a sweeping reform bill. His budget does contain important elements of tax reform—according to the Committee for a Responsible Federal Budget, the President's plan focuses on eliminating loopholes for corporations and on enacting the "Buffet Rule," which would ensure wealthy Americans pay at least 30 percent of their income in taxes.[31] The plan is not as comprehensive as those released by the deficit reduction groups, however, and focuses primarily on the tax code's progressivity.

29 "Restoring America's Future," Bipartisan Policy Center, November 2010, http://bipartisanpolicy.org/sites/default/files/files/BPC%20FINAL%20REPORT%20FOR%20PRINTER%2002%2028%2011.pdf.

30 Kelsey Snell, "Chairmen Max Baucus, Dave Camp Hit the Road to Sell Tax Reform," Politico, July 8, 2013, http://www.politico.com/story/2013/07/dave-camp-max-baucus-tax-reform-93857.html.

31 "Deficit Reduction Plan Comparison Tool," Committee for a Responsible Federal Budget, http://crfb.org/compare/side-by-side/.

Posing an even greater obstacle to reform are disputes over whether tax reform should generate revenue. Congressional Democrats want tax reform to generate revenue either to reduce the debt or to fund new investments. Congressional Republicans want tax reform to be revenue-neutral and just focused on lowering rates for taxpayers.[32] For them, keeping tax reform revenue-neutral is central to their ideology. They seek a smaller government, and earning more revenue through the tax code only ensures bigger government. Democrats aim to extract more revenue from tax reform so deficit reduction will not require as steep of spending cuts to federal programs. The revenue could also fund infrastructure improvements, new research and development, or other Democratic priorities.

Despite the proliferation of deficit reduction plans containing tax reform proposals, no progress on taxes appears imminent. The Pew Research Center duly notes the 113th Congress is "not the least productive in recent history, but close."[33] Polarization has only increased between the two parties according to the Pew study, and the political winds will not push tax reform to the forefront of the public or legislative conscience. If Congress cannot push past the question of generating revenue or not, it will be hard-pressed to dismantle popular tax expenditures. A lack of action leaves the United States with a complicated tax code that promotes horizontal and vertical inequity, inefficiency, and a growing federal debt. Americans can take heart that the fiscal cliff deal reestablished some degree of certainty to the tax code, but the compromise is not enough.

★

32 Lydia DePillis, "Six Reasons Why Tax Reform Won't Happen," The *Washington Post*, July 2, 2013, http://www.washingtonpost.com/blogs/wonkblog/wp/2013/07/02/six-reasons-why-tax-reform-wont-happen/.

33 Drew DeSilver, "Current Congress Is Not the Least Productive in Recent History, But Close," Pew Research Center, http://www.pewresearch.org/fact-tank/2013/09/03/current-congress-is-not-the-least-productive-in-recent-history-but-close/.

SOCIAL INSURANCE AND SAFETY NET: Social Security

by Daniel Backman

The Social Security program faces two conflicting truths in FY 2014: First, it needs reform. Second, reform most likely will not happen. Social Security, the New Deal program that provides direct monthly payments to retirees, their surviving dependents, and disabled workers, is the federal government's largest single annual expenditure.[34] By 2033, according to the latest projections, the program will be unable to fully pay the benefits it promises under law.[35]

At the same time, the growing cohort of American retirees and disabled workers increasingly relies on Social Security benefits to stay out of poverty. Seventy-two percent of beneficiaries in 2013 reported that without the benefits, they would be unable to afford basic shelter, food, or clothing.[36]

Yet reform remains elusive. Neither the House of Representatives' nor the Senate's budget resolution for 2014 addresses Social Security reform. Meanwhile, President Obama's 2014 budget proposal included a modest change to the way the program calculates benefits—and was quickly criticized by both the right and the left. Indeed, although a clear majority of Americans acknowledges the need to reform this popular program, even minor changes appear unlikely in the near future.[37] This apparent paradox raises the question of whether Speaker of the House Tip O'Neill's 1982 metaphor still holds: "Social Security is the third rail of American politics. Touch it, you're dead."[38]

The Problem

Social Security is a universal social insurance program, meaning it provides benefits to all U.S. citizens once they reach a certain life event—be it retirement or onset of a disability. Social Security contains two distinct programs, Old-Age and Survivors Insurance (OASI) and Disability Insurance (DI). The Social Security Administration (SSA) calculates benefits based on an indexed average of monthly earnings, and the benefits replace a greater percentage of average monthly earnings as income decreases.[39]

In 2012, about 57 million people received Social Security payments. Forty-six million retirees, their dependents, and survivors received $637.9 billion in benefits. Another $136.9 billion went to 11 million disabled workers and their dependents.[40] CBO projected total benefit outlays would increase to $809 billion in 2013, a 6 percent increase from 2012.[41]

These benefits are funded primarily by a payroll tax on labor income at a 12.4 percent rate—6.2 percent paid by the employer and 6.2 percent by the employee—up to an indexed cap of $113,700 in 2013. Eighty-five percent of these revenues go to the Old-Age and Survivors fund, and 15 percent goes toward disability insurance.[42] Payroll

34 "Historical Budget Data," Congressional Budget Office, August 2013, https://www.cbo.gov/publication/44507.
35 "The 2013 Annual Report of the Board Of Trustees of the Federal Old-Age and Survivors Insurance and Federal Disability Insurance Trust Funds," Board of Trustees, Federal Old-Age and Survivors Insurance and Federal Disability Insurance Trust Funds," May 31, 2013, http://www.ssa.gov/oact/tr/2013/tr2013.pdf.
36 Ed McCarthy, "Social Security Insecurity," LifeHealth Pro, May 28, 2013, http://www.lifehealthpro.com/2013/05/28/social-security-insecurity-how-advisors-can-help.
37 "Social Security," PollingReport.com, April 2013, http://www.pollingreport.com/social.htm.
38 William Safire, "Language: Tracking the Source of the "Third Rail" Warning," *New York Times*, February 18, 2007, http://www.nytimes.com/2007/02/18/opinion/18iht-edsafmon.4632394.html?_r=0.
39 "Social Security Benefit Amounts," Social Security Administration, accessed September 1, 2013, http://www.ssa.gov/oact/cola/Benefits.html.
40 "The 2013 Annual Report."
41 "Updated Budget Projections: Fiscal Years 2013 to 2023," Congressional Budget Office, May 2013, http://www.cbo.gov/sites/default/files/cbofiles/attachments/44172-Baseline2.pdf.
42 "Understanding the Benefits," Social Security Administration, 2013, http://ssa.gov/pubs/EN-05-10024.pdf.

tax revenues totaled $590 billion in 2012 and are projected to rise to $752 billion in 2013, primarily due to the expiration of a 2 percent payroll tax cut first passed in 2011. Social Security also receives revenues from income taxes on benefits for higher-income recipients.[43]

The OASI and DI trust funds, often considered in combination as the OASDI trust fund, make up the difference between revenues and outlays. The fund currently holds about $2.7 trillion in assets, which it uses to cover the difference between the cost of benefits and revenues for a given year. The federal government borrows from the trust fund with interest. That interest added $109 billion to the fund in 2012. Thus, the OASDI fund's assets increased by $54.4 billion in 2012.[44]

However, benefits have exceeded the fund's non-interest income (payroll and income tax revenues) since 2010, signifying a negative overall federal budget impact from Social Security, as interest income is merely a transfer from one area of the budget to another. SSA projects outlays will exceed non-interest revenues for the foreseeable future, and the cash balance of the OASDI fund will begin to fall in 2021. The OASDI trust fund will be depleted in 2033. At that point, given current law forbidding benefits in excess of revenues plus assets, Social Security will only be able to pay approximately 77 percent of scheduled benefits. This percentage would decrease slowly thereafter, reaching 72 percent in 2087.[45]

OASDI PROJECTED SPENDING AND REVENUES, 1985 - 2086

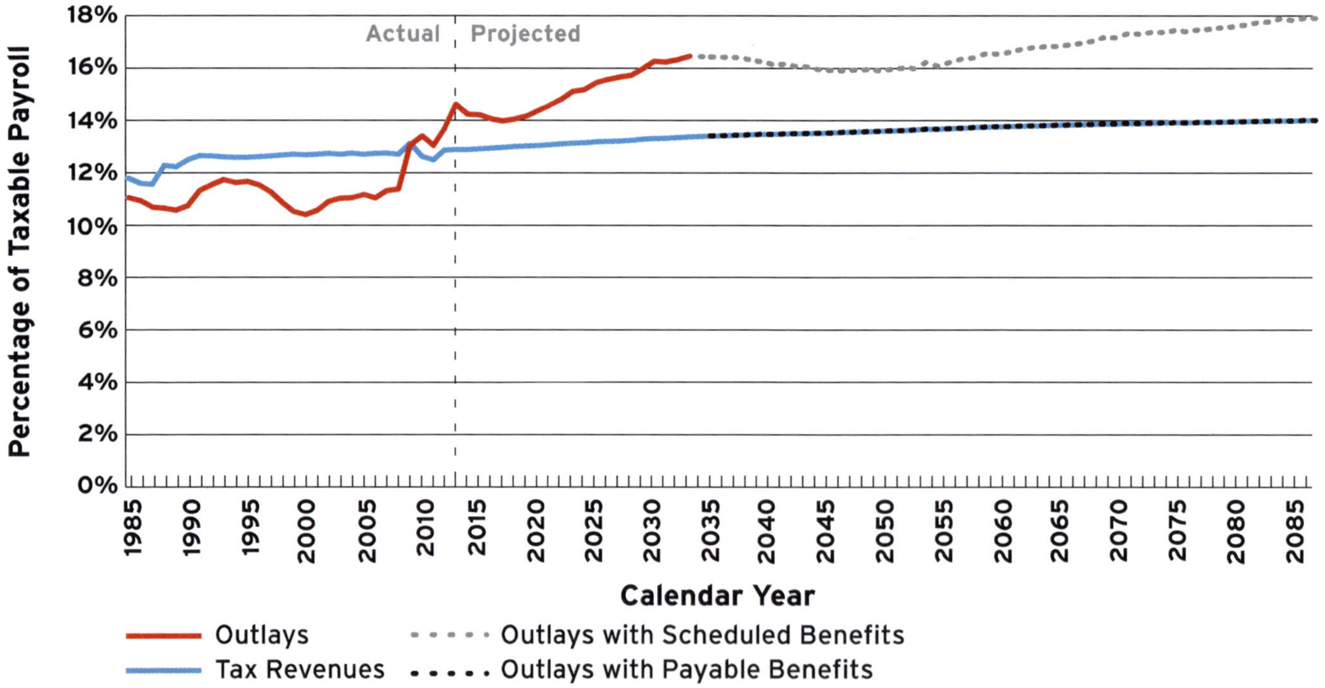

FIGURE 12 SOURCE: Congressional Budget Office, http://www.cbo.gov/sites/default/files/cbofiles/attachments/43653-2012SocialSecurityUpdate_SuppData.xls.

43 "The 2013 Annual Report."
44 Ibid.
45 Ibid.

In other words, if Social Security continues to go without reform, beneficiaries in 20 years will face a 23 percent benefit cut. By 2087, beneficiaries will receive 28 percent less than calculated under the current benefit formula.

Yet this calculation obscures the most immediate crisis in Social Security, specifically the disability program. Considered separately, the DI fund will be depleted by 2016, and the program will be able to cover only 80 percent of benefits after that date.[46] The OASI fund would be used to cover the gap until 2033, when that fund too, will run out. Any comprehensive reform of OASI must consider the unsustainable disability insurance system as well. To date, however, proposals for disability reform remain on the far back burner in Washington.

David Autor, an economist at the Massachusetts Institute of Technology and an expert on the disability insurance program, echoed this second paradox of Social Security: "There are many ways to fix the [OASI] program. The disability program, no one's talking about how to fix it, and that's a problem."[47]

SOCIAL SECURITY COSTS BY PROGRAM

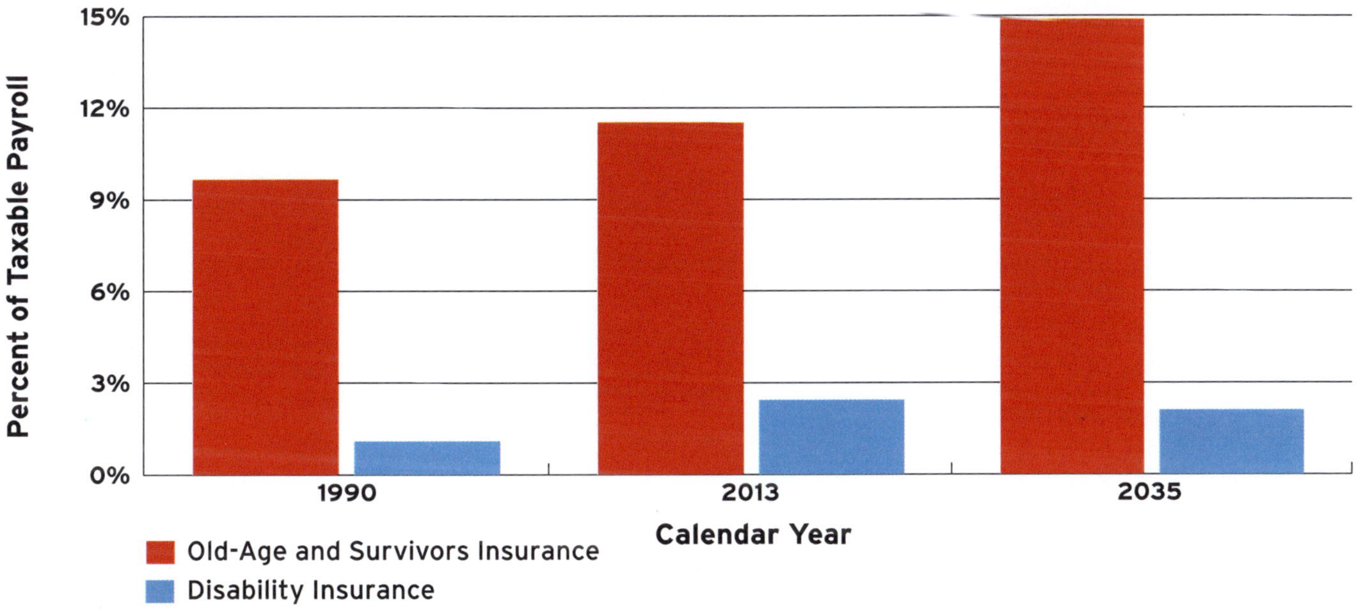

FIGURE 13 SOURCE: The Board of Trustees, Federal Old-Age and Survivors Insurance and Federal Disability Insurance Trust Funds, http://www.ssa.gov/oact/tr/2013/IV_B_LRest.html#378399.

How We Got Here

Because Social Security operates as a modified pay-as-you-go system, meaning it pays out in a given year what it receives that year, beneficiaries depend on revenues from current workers to finance the benefits they "earned" while working. Each working generation provides the benefits for the generation before it. For this reason, Social Security's sustainability depends heavily on the age distribution of the population.

46 Ibid.
47 David Autor, interview by author, August 19, 2013.

From 1974 to 2008, the ratio of workers to beneficiaries was stable, between 3.2 and 3.4. In 2012, the ratio was 2.9, a decline primarily reflecting the baby boom generation's retirement. By 2035, once most of the baby-boom generation has retired, SSA projects a ratio of 2.1, and a much more gradual decline thereafter due to increased longevity. Going forward there will be more years of receiving benefits relative to years worked. Commensurately, costs of benefits are projected to increase from 4.4 percent of GDP in 2008 to 6.2 percent in 2035 before leveling off. Revenues, meanwhile, will not surpass 4.9 percent of GDP.[48]

COVERED WORKERS PER OASDI BENEFICIARY, 1950 - 2090

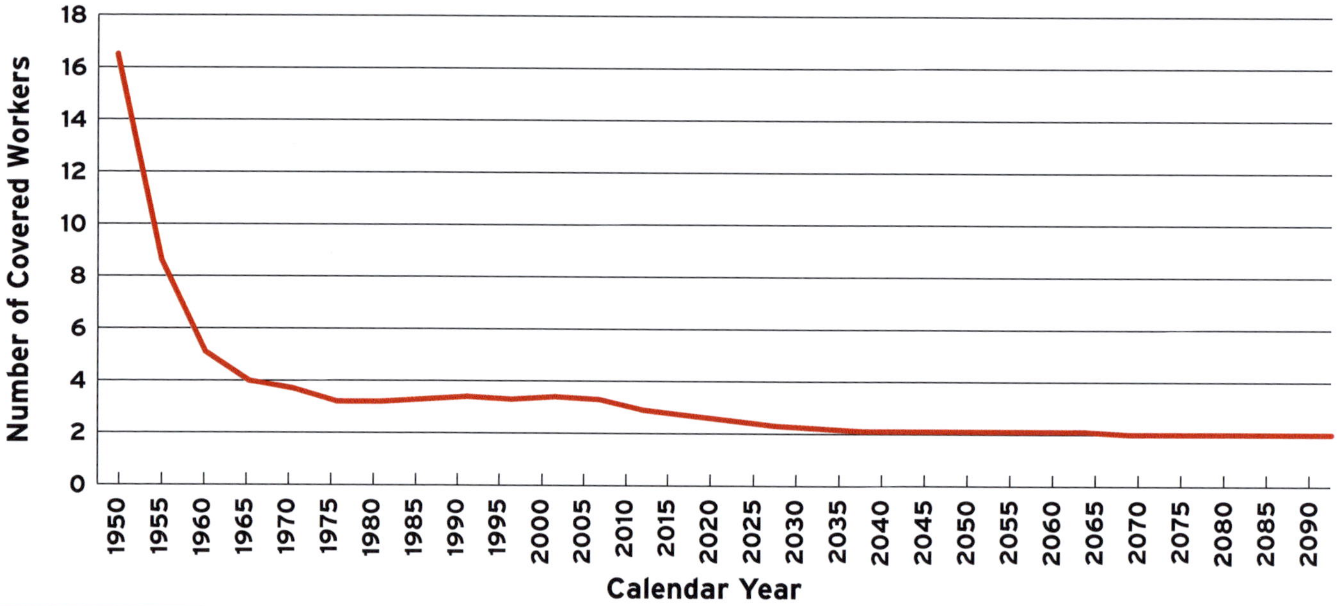

FIGURE 14 SOURCE: Board of Trustees, Federal Old-Age and Survivors Insurance and Federal Disability Insurance Trust Funds, http://www.socialsecurity.gov/oact/tr/2013/tr2013.pdf.

Yet while the aging population and its financial implications have been well documented, no effort to bridge the burgeoning gap in Social Security has passed Congress since 1983. In that year, President Reagan and Democrat Speaker O'Neill came to a bipartisan agreement that included a gradual increase in the payroll tax rate and the retirement eligibility age, a progressive income tax on benefits, and a delay in cost-of-living adjustments, among other reforms.[49] In response, SSA declared the OASDI fund "financially sound over the next 75 years."[50]

As the fund's solvency continues to shorten with passing years and updated projections, lawmakers have continually attempted and rebuffed additional reforms. In 1994, following a commission report on entitlement reform requested by President Clinton, incoming Republican House Speaker Newt Gingrich dismissed reform efforts.[51]

48 "The 2013 Annual Report."

49 "Summary of P.L. 98-21, (H.R. 1900) Social Security Amendments of 1983, Signed April 20, 1983," Social Security Administration, November 26, 1984, http://www.ssa.gov/history/1983amend.html; Paul C. Light, "The Crisis Last Time: Social Security Reform," The Brookings Institution, March 5, 2005, http://www.brookings.edu/research/opinions/2005/03/05saving-light.

50 "Summary of the 1983 Trustees Report," Social Security Administration, June 24, 1983, http://www.ssa.gov/history/pdf/1983.pdf.

51 Douglas W. Elmendorf, Jeffrey B. Liebman, and David W. Wilcox, "Fiscal Policy and Social Security Policy during the 1990s," National Bureau of Economic Research, June 2013, http://www.nber.org/papers/w8488.pdf.

In 1998, Clinton announced his "Save Social Security First" plan, in which he pledged not to enact any new tax cuts or spending increases until Social Security reform was passed. The White House and Congress debated a wide range of reform options, yet by the end of 1999, Congress had dismissed all these proposals.[52]

In 2000, candidate George W. Bush suggested transition Social Security benefits to individual private accounts, which would invest a portion of each worker's payroll taxes in stocks and bonds, while cutting traditional benefits. The reform was a centerpiece of his campaign. In 2004, he won again on a similar platform, and in 2005 he put private accounts at the center of his State of the Union address. By the fall of 2005, however, the Bush White House lost public and Congressional support for its plan, and reform once again died.[53]

The following graph shows how the 75-year Social Security trust fund projections have changed over the years, as a result of both policy changes and unanticipated economic and demographic shifts.

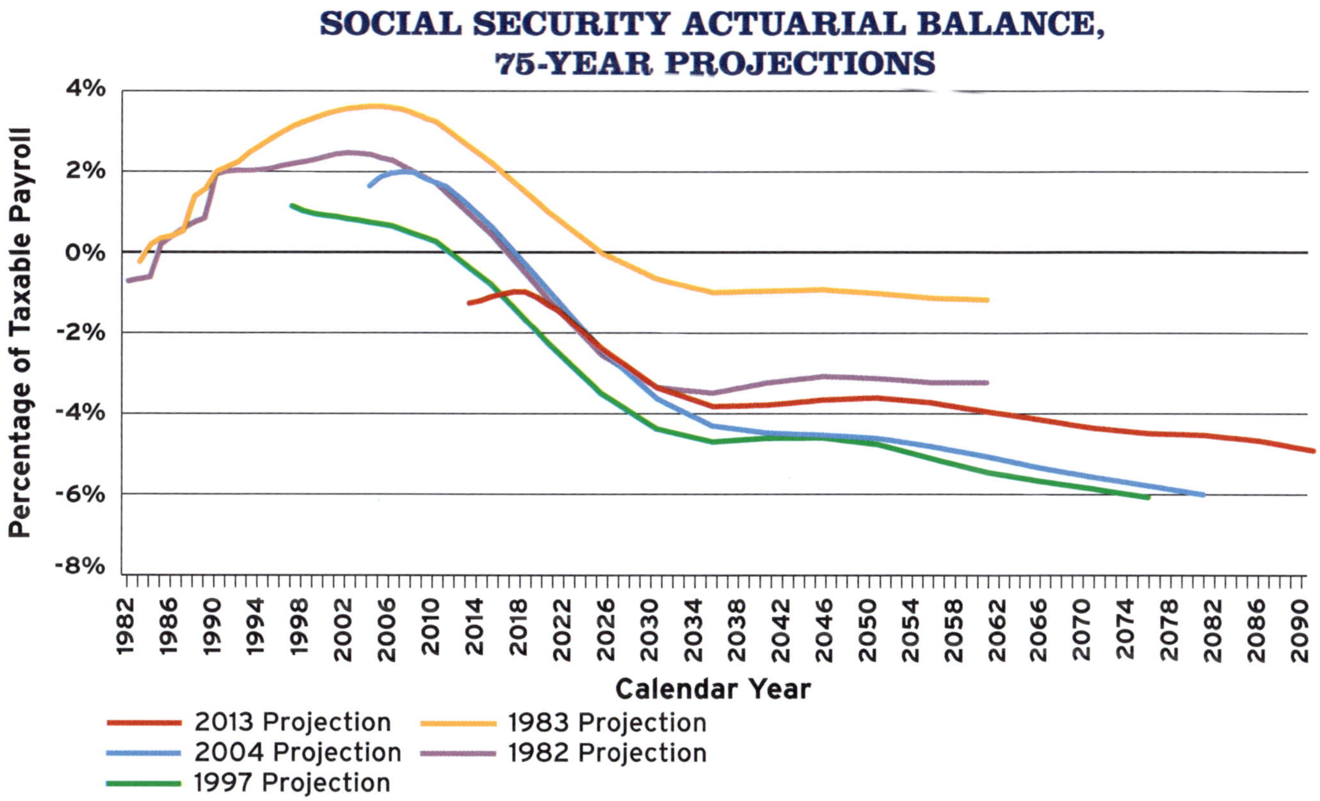

FIGURE 15

SOURCE: The Board of Trustees, Federal Old-Age and Survivors Insurance and Federal Disability Insurance Trust Funds, http://www.ssa.gov/history/reports/trust/1982/1982b.pdf, http://www.ssa.gov/history/reports/trust/1983/1983c.pdf, http://www.ssa.gov/oact/tr/TR97/tr97.pdf, http://www.ssa.gov/oact/tr/TR04/IV_LRest.html#wp257923, http://www.ssa.gov/oact/tr/2013/tr2013.pdf.

All the while, no major proposal dealt with the more immediate issue of DI insolvency. Rather, the two programs have historically been addressed separately. Yet Autor, among others, insists that the programs are so intertwined, both in their finances and operations, that any successful Social Security reform must consider both programs. Besides the fact that most assumptions of the system's solvency consider the separate funds as one, Autor points out

52 Ibid.

53 Peter Ferrara, "How George W. Bush Lost Personal Accounts for Social Security," *Forbes*, April 7, 2011, http://www.forbes.com/sites/peterferrara/2011/04/07/how-george-w-bush-lost-personal-accounts-for-social-security/.

that OASI reforms, like the rising retirement age enacted in the 1983 act, have merely shifted some beneficiaries onto DI. Basically, says Autor, it gives these workers "an early retirement, without the penalty of retiring early." This has increased costs to the DI system.[54]

Autor and others—including think-tanks such as the Center for American Progress, the Brookings Institution, and the Heritage Foundation—have called for a debate on DI reform because the problem extends beyond OASI's aging-population dilemma.[55] As Mark Duggan, professor of business economics and public policy at the University of Pennsylvania, put it, "This is a program that is crying out for reform."[56]

According to Autor, population growth, population aging, and increased female participation in the labor force explains only about 50 percent of the rise in disability roles since the early 1990s. The other half stems from increased eligibility for and dependence on disability within a given age and gender group, even as the population has grown healthier. At this point, about 5 percent of Americans age 25 to 64 receives DI benefits.[57]

Yet Autor claims that past DI reforms have either made little impact on the program's funding or exacerbated the problem. In particular, Autor claims that the 1996 efforts to eliminate drug and alcohol addiction as an eligible disability had little impact, as most of the 210,000 beneficiaries kicked off the system became eligible in other ways. Other reforms intended to incentivize reentry into the labor force, he wrote, had little impact. Further, he cites a 1984 reform that liberalized eligibility, and thus increased the number of disability beneficiaries, as a key contributor to the program's unsustainability.[58]

Duggan broadly agrees with this assessment. He also points out that stagnant median incomes have led to more workers falling into the highest replacement rate category. For more and more workers, disability insurance will replace 90 percent of their income.[59] Finally, he cites the appeals process as a cause for heightened generosity of benefits. At these hearings, he told ARUSA in an interview, administrative judges overrule the Social Security Administration's decision to reject the applicant 72 percent of the time. He ascribes this to the fact that the judge only hears the applicant's side while the SSA has no representation at the hearing.[60]

Proposals for Reform

As mentioned, the budget debates of 2013 included few proposals for Social Security reform. The most prominent was President Obama's "Chained CPI" proposal, which he included in his 2014 budget based on an offer made to House of Representatives Speaker John Boehner in December 2012.[61] This measure would change the way inflation is calculated in determining how much to increase benefits each year once a beneficiary reaches retirement. Although experts debate whether this new inflation measure more accurately represents the prices seniors face, no

54 David Autor, interview by author, August 19, 2013.
55 David H. Autor and Mark Duggan, "Supporting Work: A Proposal for Modernizing the U.S. Disability Insurance System," Center for American Progress, December 2010, http://www.americanprogress.org/wp-content/uploads/issues/2010/12/pdf/autordugganpaper.pdf; Jeffrey B. Liebman and Jack A. Smalligan, "An Evidence-Based Path to Disability Insurance Reform," The Brookings Institution, February 26, 2013, http://www.brookings.edu/research/papers/2013/02/disability-insurance-reform; James Sherk, "Not Looking for Work: Why Labor Force Participation Has Fallen During the Recession," Heritage Foundation, August 2012, http://www.heritage.org/research/reports/2013/09/not-looking-for-work-why-labor-force-participation-has-fallen-during-the-recession.
56 Mark Duggan, interview by author, August 30, 2013.
57 David H. Autor, "The Unsustainable Rise of the Disability Rolls in the United States: Causes, Consequences, and Policy Options," Massachusetts Institute of Technology, November 23, 2011, http://economics.mit.edu/files/7388.
58 Ibid.
59 Mark Duggan, "The Rise in SSDI Enrollment, the Impact on the Labor Market, and the Need for Reform," Testimony before the Subcommittee on Social Security of the Committee on Ways and Means," U.S. House of Representatives, June 19, 2013, http://waysandmeans.house.gov/uploadedfiles/duggan_testimony_61913ss.pdf.
60 Mark Duggan, interview by author, August 30, 2013.
61 "Chained CPI Protections," Office of Management and Budget, April 2013, http://www.whitehouse.gov/omb/budget/factsheet/chained-cpi-protections.

one denies that this change would decrease benefits for current and future recipients. The White House estimates that this change will reduce deficits by $230 billion over 10 years.[62] And the Social Security Administration projected the change would put off the trust fund's depletion by one year.[63]

According to the Center for Economic and Policy Research, switching to Chained CPI would decrease the average worker's annual benefits by $650 by age 75 and $1,130 by age 85.[64] The Obama administration sought to address this critique by including a 5 percent benefit enhancement starting 15 years after retirement.[65]

Additionally, the lower inflation adjustment would increase income tax revenues by decreasing the rate at which the tax bracket cutoffs increase. CEPR finds that 69 percent of the additional revenue would come from taxpayers earning less than $100,000 a year. Specifically, the tax burden on taxpayers earning between $10,000 and $20,000 per year would increase by 14.5 percent, while increasing the tax burden on those making over $1 million by only 0.1 percent.[66]

Liberals immediately jumped on this proposal as a betrayal to seniors already struggling to survive on Social Security benefits, and as a tax increase on the middle class. MoveOn.org, a progressive advocacy group, called on its membership to "mobilize and stop this attempt to diminish the vital guarantee of Social Security," comparing Obama's proposal to Bush's privatization plans.[67] Senator Bernie Sanders (I-Vt.), the social democratic independent from Vermont, accused the president of breaking his promises not to reduce the deficit "on the backs of" the elderly, poor, and disabled.[68] Major conservative groups, meanwhile, criticized the proposal for its tax increases. Still, some conservatives applauded the president for proposing entitlement reform at all.[69]

The other major reform hanging over debates in Washington has not actually been proposed since 2010. Rep. Paul Ryan's 2011 budget resolution, which House Republicans passed in 2010, included a partial privatization scheme that Republicans have since dropped. The main thrust of the plan established voluntary individual accounts, similar to the Bush plan of 2005, which Ryan also helped author. Under this program, each taxpayer under age 55 could choose to divert a portion of his or her payroll taxes into a private account invested 65 percent in stocks and 35 percent in corporate bonds. For those who chose to use these accounts, traditional Social Security benefits would decrease proportionally to the payroll taxes diverted from the Social Security trust fund into the personal accounts.[70]

The Social Security Administration found that Ryan's reforms, which also include reductions for higher-income recipients, indexing the retirement age to increases in average life expectancy, and limited revenue increases, would keep the trust fund solvent through 2083.[71] However, Democrats widely criticized the proposal as a privatization

62 "Reducing the Deficit in a Smart and Balanced Way," Office of Management and Budget, April 2013, http://www.whitehouse.gov/sites/default/files/omb/budget/fy2014/assets/reducing.pdf.
63 "Financial Effects on Social Security of Two changes in the President's Fiscal Year 2014 Budget," Social Security Administration, July 11, 2013, http://www.ssa.gov/oact/solvency/FY2014Budget_20130711.pdf.
64 Alan Barber and Nicole Woo, "The Chained CPI: A Painful Cut in Social Security Benefits and a Stealth Tax Hike," Center for Economic and Policy Research," December 2012, http://www.cepr.net/documents/publications/cpi-2012-12.pdf.
65 Ibid.
66 Ibid.
67 Brett Logiurato, "Liberals Are Already Freaking Out Over the Obama Budget's Social Security Cuts," Business Insider, April 5, 2013, http://www.businessinsider.com.au/chained-cpi-social-security-cuts-obama-budget-liberals-move-on-aarp-2013-4.
68 "Sanders Statement on Obama Cuts in Social Security, Veterans Benefits, Office of Sen. Bernie Sanders, April 5, 2013, http://www.sanders.senate.gov/newsroom/press-releases/sanders-statement-on-obama-cuts-in-social-security-veterans-benefits.
69 Bernie Becker, "Club for Growth, Norquist Warn of Tax Hikes from Chained CPI," The Hill, April 29, 2013, http://thehill.com/blogs/on-the-money/domestic-taxes/296745-conservative-groups-oppose-chained-cpi-as-tax-proposal.
70 "Financial Effects of H.R. 4529," Social Security Administration, April 27, 2010, http://www.ssa.gov/oact/solvency/PRyan_20100427.pdf.
71 Ibid.

of Social Security, or a return to the Bush proposals, seen as a major reason for Democrats retaking Congress in 2006. Indeed, Democrats attempted to tie Ryan and Mitt Romney to the Bush plan, and thus to President Bush, in the 2012 election. Yet Romney rejected the plan, and Republicans have since dropped it from their annual budget resolutions.[72]

Still the "Third Rail" of Politics?

Few question the premise that Social Security will require reform in the near future. Politicians on both sides of the aisle have put forward proposals that either increase revenues or cut benefits to the Old-Age and Survivors Insurance program and the Disability Insurance program. Some, like House Republicans in 2010, have put forward more fundamental reforms. Yet none of these proposals looks likely to pass in the current political environment. In that sense, Social Security may still be the third rail of politics.

Yet the political debate obscures the fact that public opinion may lie narrowly on the side of reform. Fifty-one percent of Americans, according to a Bloomberg National Poll from February 2013, think a "major overhaul" of Social Security will be necessary to reduce the deficit, compared to 31 percent who disagree. In that same poll, 64 percent declared support for reducing benefit increases. However, when asked in an *ABC News/Washington Post* poll about Obama's Chained CPI proposal, only 37 percent supported it.[73] Such results suggest that Social Security reform may be possible, if sold the right way.

Until then, significant reforms to Social Security are nowhere on the political horizon.

★

72 Stephen Ohlemacher, "Social Security Privatization Fight Revived by Dems to Attack Paul Ryan," *Huffington Post*, August 19, 2012, http://www.huffingtonpost.com/2012/08/19/social-security-privatization-paul-ryan_n_1806309.html.

73 "Social Security," PollingReport.com, April 2013, http://www.pollingreport.com/social.htm.

SOCIAL INSURANCE AND SAFETY NET: Health Care

by Matt Shuham

The Affordable Care Act is very, very complicated. Let's just say that again…very, very complicated. Not just complicated because the bill that passed through Congress was thousands of pages long, or because it will take years and thousands of highly trained administrators to make sure it's implemented correctly, but complicated because it's transforming the largest industry in America—health care. ACA is legislation that will fundamentally change America, but for now, years after it was passed, economists and reporters are having hard enough of a time tracking the law through its implementation phase and how it will affect fiscal sustainability. As Ricardo Alonso-Zaldivar of the *Associated Press* noted, the federal budget doesn't even have a chapter labeled "The Affordable Care Act," let alone an in-depth analysis of how exactly the bill will affect America's budget.[74]

At its core, the law is a fulfillment of one of President Obama's biggest campaign promises: making sure every American has quality health care. It's important to note that the president never pledged to provide health care to cvery American that wanted it. In fact, the entire legislation depends on young, healthy people enrolling in health care plans (whether they want to or not) in order tu provide insurance companies the extra money to cover those who really need it. This "mandate" on young people, among others, is crucial for the law's solvency.

Because they received a new crop of clients, insurance companies were willing to make important concessions. Now, young people can stay on their parents' plans until they reach 26 years old and no one can be denied coverage due to a pre-existing conditions. The Affordable Care Act also included an expansion of the Medicaid program, which gives money to states in order to provide basic insurance to low-income individuals and families. This would have completed a huge shift in the health care ecosystem in the United States: after reaching out to younger people and ensuring the sick could be covered, the poor would find solace in increased government insurance. But, when the Supreme Court ruled on the Affordable Care Act last summer, Medicaid expansion was left, so to speak, on the court floor. Instead of the expansion becoming a cornerstone of the health care plan, the court ordered that states ought to have a choice of whether to accept the national money and the administrative work that came with it.

This is where ARUSA picks up the story today: America has decades of debate over health care, and now she must assemble a new national picture of health coverage. The law has passed and has been deemed constitutional, but implementation is just beginning.

Convincing Millennials

Convincing young people that buying insurance is worth it for them is a deceivingly simple-seeming aspect of the Obama health care plan. In June, President Obama began a publicity tour that brought him around the country pitching his plan to a waiting nation. He spoke with urgency to the millions Americans between 18 and 35 years old without health insurance: He wants 2.5 million of them to enroll in new insurance plans.[75] For his plan to work, they would have to see that health care coverage was worth the cost, at least more than the fine they would pay if they didn't enroll. Helping the president in his effort was a major aspect of the plan: online insurance marketplaces that offered subsidized insurance in each state to the uninsured. In theory, the marketplaces would

74 Ricardo Alonzo-Zaldivar, "Costs of Obamacare Sprinkled Across Hundreds of Pages of Obama's 2014 Budget," *Christian Science Monitor*, April 13, 2013, http://cnsnews.com/news/article/costs-obamacare-sprinkled-across-hundreds-pages-obamas-2014-budget.

75 Mallory Sfastaii, "With Open Enrollment on Horizon, Young People Key to Obamacare's Success," PBS Newshour, August 13, 2013, http://www.pbs.org/newshour/rundown/2013/08/young-people-are-key-to-obamacare.html.

make it easier for the uninsured—especially those born and raised in the Internet age—to access affordable care, broaden the risk pool in their plan, lower premiums for everyone, and avoid punitive taxes, which started at $95 in 2014 and increase to 2.5 percent of annual income in 2016. Their payments into insurance might be thought of as paying for something they don't need, or at least not yet. Healthy young people paying insurance premiums would cover the increased cost to insurance companies of covering the many older and sicker people that would sign up anew for insurance, knowing this time that it would be illegal for them to be turned away for a pre-existing condition.

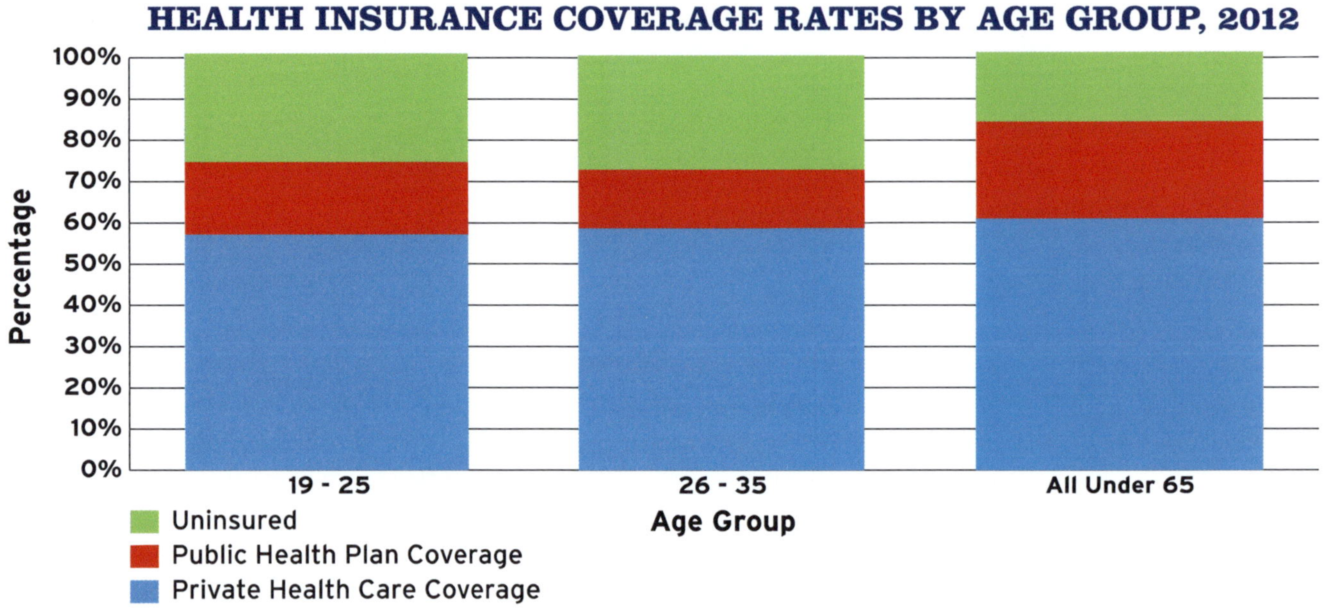

FIGURE 16 SOURCE: Centers for Disease Control and Prevention, http://www.cdc.gov/nchs/data/nhis/earlyrelease/insur201306.pdf.

Observers can trace the cost of these subsidized state insurance marketplaces and see if they are financially feasible. According to *Reuters*, the marketing campaign targeted towards young adults cost in the hundreds of millions of dollars and became part of the budget of the Department of Health and Human Services.[76] In the administration's eyes, it was a small price to pay if it ultimately drove millions of young people to sign up for coverage. The president also apparently received some pro bono help from comedians around the country, in PSAs and comedy videos reminiscent of the Ad Council's old World War II announcements.[77]

Despite the dissemination effort, there's still plenty of work to do if the president wants to shore up this aspect of his health plan: Surveys show that, although young people recognize the importance of having health care, they still view it as cost prohibitive. Even after the president hit the stump, only 1 in 4 young people knew what state health exchanges were.[78] And considering up to 82 percent uninsured young people in the U.S. would qualify for federal or state assistance, according to the *Insurance Journal*, it begs the question: if more young people knew

76 David Morgan, "Final Obamacare push will pitch to the low-income young," *Reuters* US, June 14, 2013, http://www.reuters.com/article/2013/06/14/us-usa-healthcare-outreach-idUSBRE95D13620130614.

77 Roberta Rampton, "A Potent New Force in Selling Obamacare to Youth," The *Fiscal Times*, July 23, 2013, http://www.thefiscaltimes.com/Articles/2013/07/23/The-Potent-New-Force-in-Selling-Obamacare-to-Youth.aspx#page1.

78 "Kaiser Health Tracking Poll: June 2013," Kaiser Family Foundation, June 19, 2013, http://kff.org/health-reform/poll-finding/kaiser-health-tracking-poll-june-2013/.

about health exchanges and other financial aids, would they more buy insurance? It's possible that this key part of financing health insurance reform will fall flat, due in part to ineffective messaging.

Expanding Medicaid

In their 2012 decision on the constitutionality of the Affordable Care Act, the Supreme Court essentially rendered one aspect of it optional for states: acceptance of federal Medicaid dollars for use on low income individuals' and families' health care needs.[79] The federal government, the court ruled, could not pressure states to accept federal funds. Acceptance had to be on a state's terms.

That dramatic turn in the massive law's course put some agency back in the hands of states when it came to implementation. State health exchanges also empowered states. Now, governors and state legislatures across the country had to decide if it was worth it for their state to accept federal money for Medicaid expansion.

STATE MEDICAID EXPANSION DECISIONS AS OF DECEMBER, 2013

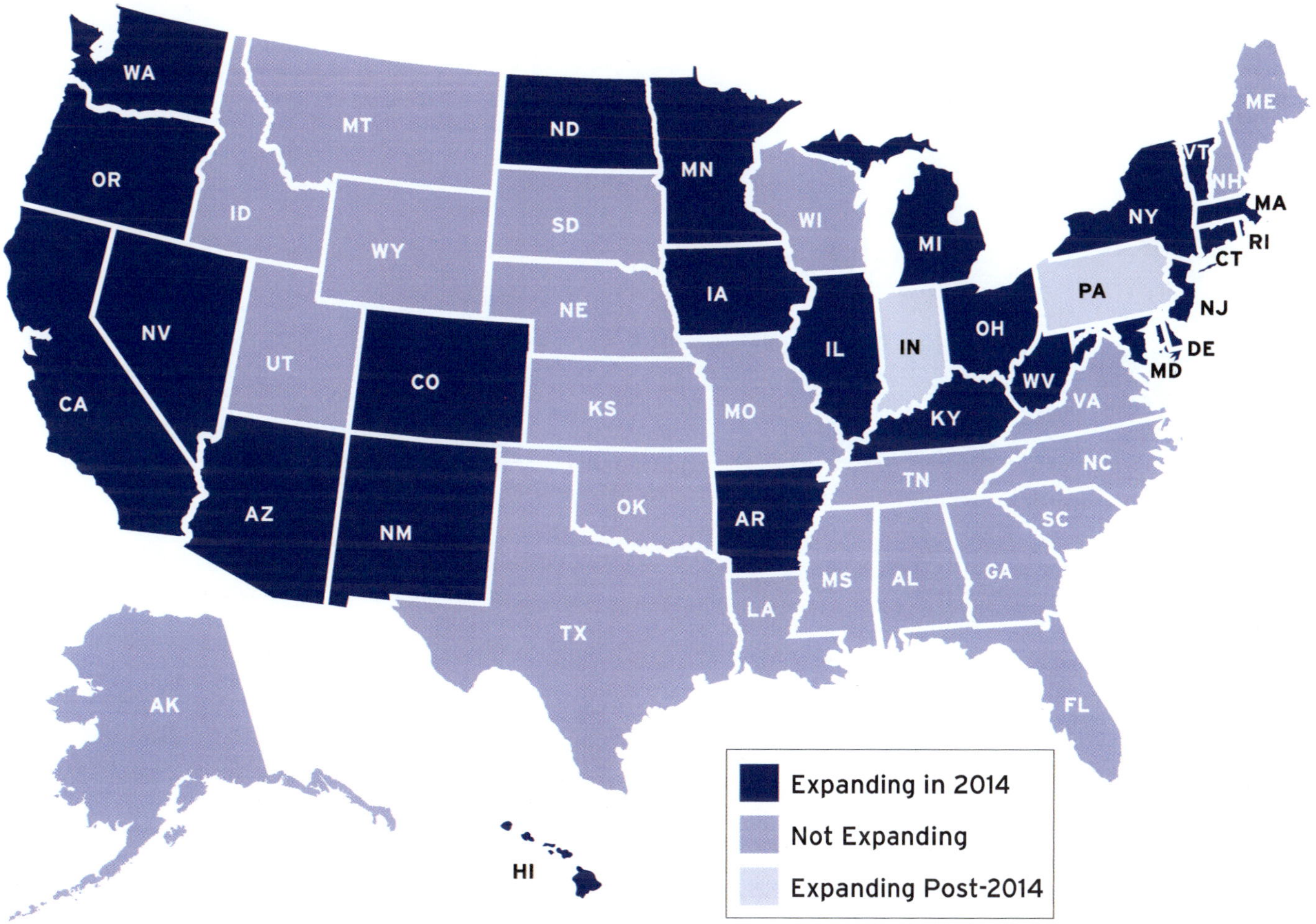

FIGURE 17 SOURCE: Kaiser Family Foundation, http://kaiserfamilyfoundation.files.wordpress.com/2013/01/8384_es.pdf, http://kff.org/medicaid/state-indicator/state-activity-around-expanding-medicaid-under-the-affordable-care-act/#map.

79 "A Guide to the Supreme Court's Decision on the ACA's Medicaid Expansion," Kaiser Family Foundation, August 1, 2013, http://kff.org/health-reform/issue-brief/a-guide-to-the-supreme-courts-decision/.

TABLE 2 - FEDERAL AND STATE BUDGETARY EFFECTS OF MEDICAID EXPANSION, 2013 - 2022 (millions of dollars)

State	Federal Budget Cost	State Budget Cost	State	Federal Budget Cost	State Budget Cost
Alabama	$14,371	$1,081	Montana	$2,088	$194
Alaska	$1,458	$147	Nebraska	$3,063	$250
Arizona	$10,701	$467	Nevada	$5,620	$513
Arkansas	$12,465	$922	New Hampshire	$2,417	$188
California	$68,750	$6,314	New Jersey	$15,366	$1,492
Colorado	$10,308	$858	New Mexico	$4,926	$268
Connecticut	$8,159	-$1,251	New York	$56,107	-$33,345
Delaware	$1,927	-$1,100	North Carolina	$3,9638	$3,075
District of Columbia	$852	$67	North Dakota	$2,357	$211
Florida	$66,113	$5,364	Ohio	$43,341	$4,017
Georgia	$33,711	$2,541	Oklahoma	$8,561	$689
Hawaii	$3,294	-$340	Oregon	$12,842	$506
Idaho	$3,280	$246	Pennsylvania	$37,842	$2,842
Illinois	$21,756	$2,213	Rhode Island	$2,935	$250
Indiana	$17,322	$1,099	South Carolina	$15,827	$1,155
Iowa	$3,909	-$534	South Dakota	$2,110	$157
Kansas	$5,270	$525	Tennessee	$22,541	$1,715
Kentucky	$17,832	$1,297	Texas	$65,619	$5,669
Louisiana	$15,786	$1,244	Utah	$5,274	$364
Maine	$3,124	-$570	Vermont	$1,026	-$886
Maryland	$12,253	-$1,751	Virginia	$14,665	$1,326
Massachusetts	$7,270	-$6,617	Washington	$8,406	$121
Michigan	$17,512	$1,661	West Virginia	$8,744	$619
Minnesota	$5,597	$472	Wisconsin	$12,263	-$248
Mississippi	$14,499	$1,048	Wyoming	$1,353	$118
Missouri	$17,795	$1,573			

SOURCE: http://kaiserfamilyfoundation.files.wordpress.com/2013/01/8384_es.pdf.

But what about the decision is so hard? The Affordable Care Act calls for Medicaid expansion for individuals and families living up to 133 percent of the poverty line—all state governments have to do is accept the free federal money. Rejecting the money, meanwhile, carries a slew of downsides. Ezra Klein summed it up nicely: "[A study by the Rand Corporation] looks at the 14 states that have said they will opt out of the new Medicaid funds.[80] It finds that the result will be they get $8.4 billion less in federal funding, have to spend an extra $1 billion in uncompensated care, and end up with about 3.6 million fewer insured residents."[81]

So, why are so many states rejecting Medicaid expansion money?

80 Carter Price and Christine Eibner, "For States That Opt Out Of Medicaid Expansion: 3.6 Million Fewer Insured And $8.4 Billion Less In Federal Payments," *Health Affairs*, June 4, 2013, http://content.healthaffairs.org/content/32/6/1030.abstract.

81 Ezra Klein and Evan Soltas, "The terrible deal for states rejecting Medicaid," The *Washington Post*, June 4, 2013, http://www.washingtonpost.com/blogs/wonkblog/wp/2013/06/04/wonkbook-the-terrible-deal-for-states-rejecting-medicaid/.

TABLE 3 - SELECTED STATE COSTS DUE TO MEDICAID EXPANSION, 2013 - 2022 (millions of dollars)

State	Expansion Status	Governor's Party	State Costs	State Costs Per New Enrollee
Alabama	No	Republican	$1,081	$3,454
Arkansas	Yes	Democrat	$922	$3,957
California	Yes	Democrat	$6,314	$3,395
Georgia	No	Republican	$2,541	$3,640
Louisiana	No	Republican	$1,244	$3,126
New Hampshire	No	Democrat	$188	$4,476
New Jersey	Yes	Republican	$1,492	$5,127
New York	Yes	Democrat	-$33,345	-$104,203
Ohio	Yes	Republican	$4,017	$5,873
Tennessee	No	Republican	$1,715	$4,725
Texas	No	Republican	$5,669	$3,141

SOURCE: http://kaiserfamilyfoundation.files.wordpress.com/2013/01/8384.pdf.

For one, states *will* eventually have to pay some of the expanded Medicaid's bill. While federal funds cover 100 percent of the expansion, states will have to pay 5 percent of the total starting in 2017, and 10 percent after 2020. Some governors announced their intent to veto any Medicaid expansion money on these grounds, but for others, it was a matter of principle, a protest of what they viewed as a harmful, wasteful law. In most states where this was the case, bills to accept federal funding died in the legislature without much fuss. It was a closed case, in some cases over the objections of would-be Medicaid recipients.[82]

Granted, this isn't exactly a partisan split: Republicans like Jan Brewer of Arizona and Chris Christie of New Jersey have pledged to expand Medicaid on the federal government's terms. Still, the states rejecting funding are overwhelmingly red. Most Democrat-controlled states, meanwhile, jumped at the chance to receive more federal funding. Many requested permission to expand Medicaid before the Supreme Court even ruled on it.[83]

Did all of these states rejecting federal money save the federal government money? Rick Perry articulated the view of many conservative state lawmakers who believed that it was their job not to add to the federal deficit: "They tell us to take the money—in the case of Texas, $4 billion—because it's free," Perry said in a speech on March 14 in Washington. "But there is nothing free. This is our money, or at least money that we've tacked onto the national debt either by borrowing from China or by pulling it right off the printing presses."

However, there are ramifications for these decisions. Larry Levitt, Senior Vice President for Special Initiatives at the Kaiser Family Foundation, said in an interview with ARUSA that such a decision could impact small businesses. "[In states without expanded ACA Medicaid] some of those lower wage workers would likely opt to apply to Medicaid rather than apply in their employer plan, which saves their employers money. So not going ahead with the Medicaid expansion may translate to higher costs for larger employers."[84]

82 "Where the States Stand on Medicaid," The Advisory Board Company, February 7, 2014, http://www.advisory.com/Daily-Briefing/Resources/Primers/MedicaidMap.
83 Ibid.
84 Larry Levitt, interview with author, September 5, 2013.

The Big Business Delay

Beyond young people and state governments, there's another force in American health care economics that's driving the story behind Obamacare's implementation: businesses. Specifically, this is in regards to the so-called "employer mandate," which specified that companies with 50 or more full-time employees must provide them a health care plan.

The employer mandate was a big sticking point for many in the business community, and many Republicans, during the original health care debates. Employers and business organizations such as the Chamber of Commerce argued that the health care requirement would force businesses to artificially reduce payroll numbers. They also argued that it would depress hiring for every employee after number 50 and create market distortions towards part-time labor, one of the primary pests of the 2008 recession.[85]

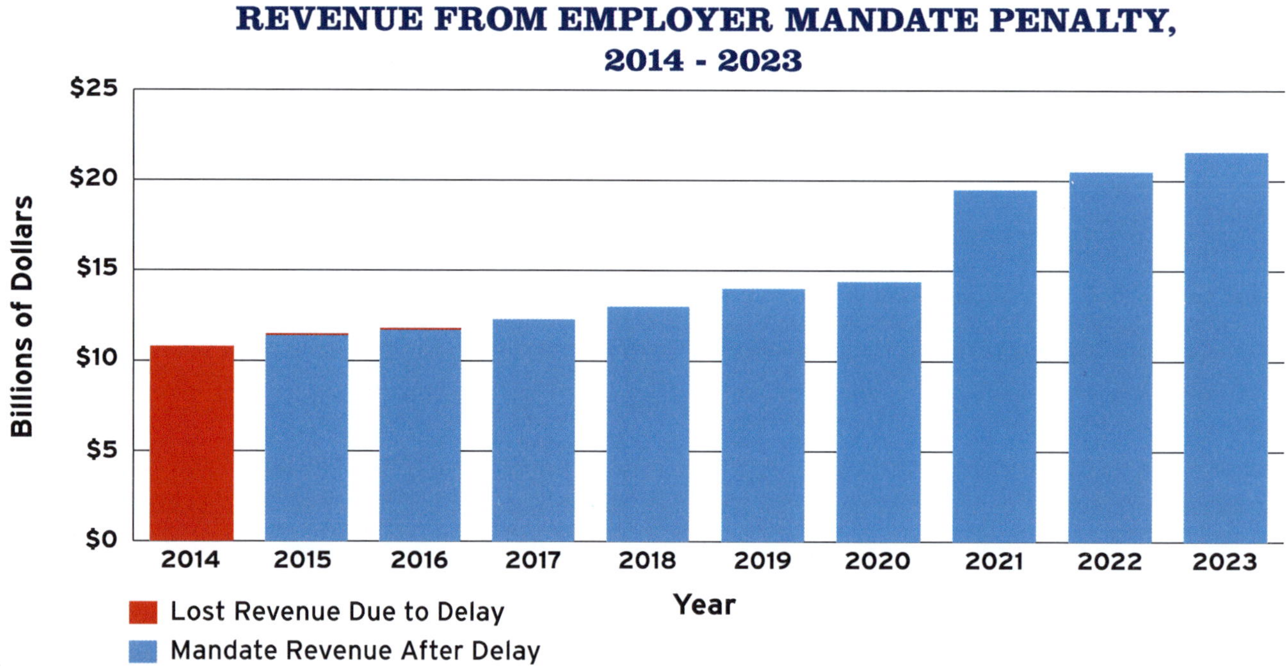

FIGURE 18 SOURCE: RAND Corporation, http://www.rand.org/content/dam/rand/pubs/research_reports/RR400/RR411/RAND_RR411.pdf.

These apprehensions didn't go away when the 4th Circuit Court of Appeals upheld the employer mandate as constitutional, nor were fears assuaged as the impending deadline for the requirement, in 2014, approached with an ominous speed.[86] Heck, even White Castle Hamburgers, that ever-expanding signpost of economic well-being, stopped building new restaurants, citing uncertainty over the future of health care and hiring practices.[87] So, the president delayed the employer mandate for a year.[88]

85 "Employer Mandate," U.S. Chamber of Commerce, http://www.uschamber.com/health-reform/employer-mandate.

86 Paul Davidson, "Health care law may mean less hiring in 2013," *USA Today*, December 30, 2012, http://www.usatoday.com/story/money/business/2012/12/30/health-care-law-jobs/1785641/.

87 Sally Pipes, "Delay of Obamacare's Employer Mandate Exacerbates An Already Bad Situation," *Forbes*, August 5, 2013, http://www.forbes.com/sites/sallypipes/2013/08/05/delay-of-obamacares-employer-mandate-exacerbates-an-already-bad-situation/.

88 Mark Mazur, "Continuing to Implement the ACA in a Careful, Thoughtful Manner," Department of the Treasury, July 2, 2013, http://www.treasury.gov/connect/blog/pages/continuing-to-implement-the-aca-in-a-careful-thoughtful-manner-.aspx.

This was a significant political decision: President Obama lost some of the credibility he had maintained by claiming throughout the implementation process that Obamacare was on track and proceeding according to his administration's expectations. Delaying a major portion of the bill for a year did not exactly echo that message. It gave some credence to the Republican claims that the health care overhaul was more trouble than it was worth.

But there were budgetary implications, as well: even though big business will be given a year extra to avoid paying for employee health care, individuals will still have to comply with the individual mandate. This means that a low-income individual that might have been covered by their business' new insurance requirement will now have to be covered by either expanded Medicaid at the state level, or federal subsidies and assistance. This will add millions, maybe billions, of dollars to federal health care expenses, instead of spreading those costs across the private sector. Many conservatives are probably happy for this temporary shift: private businesses keep more of their money. Still, in the long run, this will likely add to the deficit.

What Now?

It's difficult to write about the Affordable Care Act. It's difficult even to think about the Affordable Care Act, and especially difficult if you're a governor, or any part of the state-level administrations around the country tasked with actually implementing the bill. In fact, the bill is remarkably self-aware in this respect. Here comes the ground-level elbow grease of health care reform: navigators.

Health care navigators are unbiased professional organizations paid by the government to offer their free services in helping people enroll in health care. They're there to navigate the process with people, providing, ironically, a government-subsidized guide through the government bureaucracy of health care. In other words, they exist to make the ACA work.

More than a hundred groups were collectively given $67 million in grants to act as regional navigators. This may seem like a paltry sum in comparison to the vastness of the bill, especially given the mammoth job these groups are tasked with. In the months ahead, they will be working to explain to the American people, block by block and one information session at a time, about the rules of "Obamacare." Their work is daunting and may go unnoticed, but for everything else to work they must not miss a beat.

★

by Daniel Backman

Health care expenditures presented a daunting challenge to the federal budget in 2013 and the years beyond. In 2012, taxpayers paid about $802 billion to fund Medicare and Medicaid, the two largest federal health care programs. That amounts to 23 percent of total federal spending and about 5 percent of U.S. economic output.[89] [90] By 2023, these two programs combined will pay out $1.62 trillion, or 6.2 percent of GDP.[91] Simply put, when people talk about the United States' deficit problem, they should be talking about the cost of these two programs.

MEDICARE AND MEDICAID EXPENDITURES, 1973 - 2013

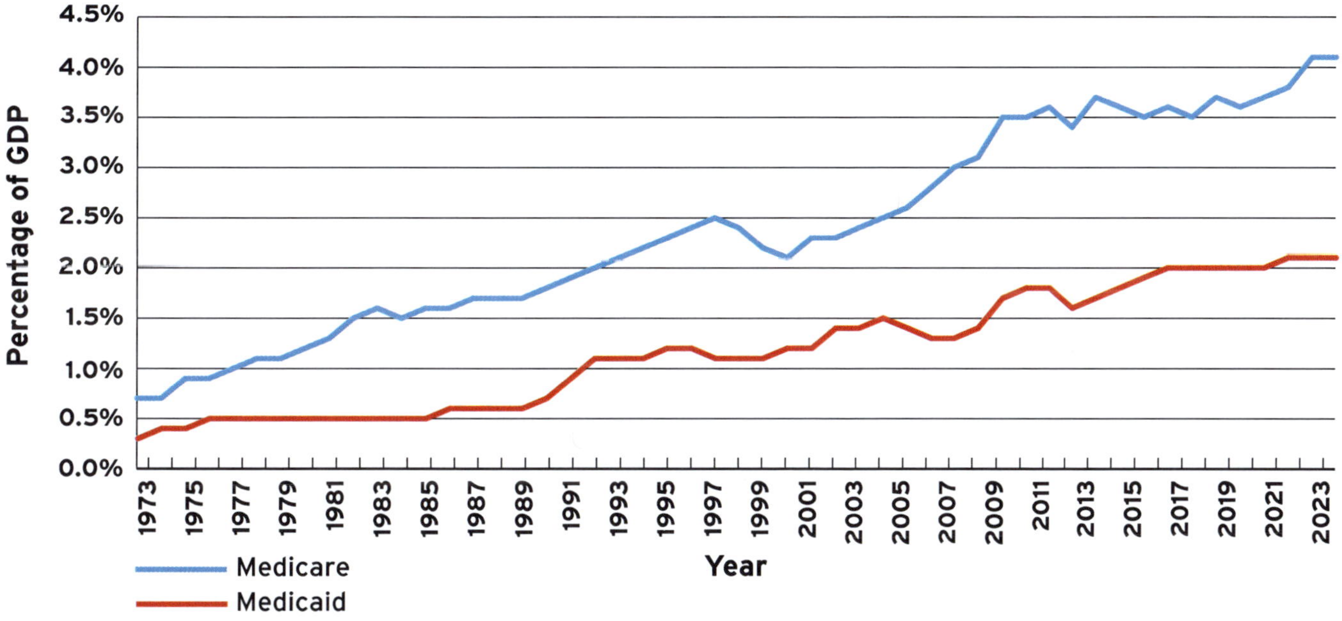

FIGURE 19 SOURCE: Congressional Budget Office, https://www.cbo.gov/sites/default/files/cbofiles/attachments/HistoricalBudgetData_Aug13.xls and http://www.cbo.gov/sites/default/files/cbofiles/attachments/44172-Baseline2.pdf.

But while Medicare and Medicaid often get discussed as a pair, their purposes and functions diverge considerably. Though enacted simultaneously by President Lyndon B. Johnson under the Social Security Amendments of 1965, Medicare was designed as a universal social insurance program, providing expansive health care services to seniors and the disabled regardless of means.[92] Medicaid, on the other hand, is a means-tested welfare program that provides basic health services to low-income Americans.[93] In addition, whereas the federal government administers the mostly standardized Medicare benefits to all those eligible throughout the country, individual states operate the Medicaid program subject to minimum federal standards and aided by federal cost-sharing.[94]

As two of the largest so-called entitlement programs, along with Social Security, Medicare and Medicaid reform lies at the center of many deficit-cutting proposals. The Affordable Care Act of 2010 implemented changes to both

89 "Historical Budget Data," Congressional Budget Office, August 2013, https://www.cbo.gov/publication/44507.
90 This figure does not include the state-funded portion of Medicaid.
91 "Updated Budget Projections: Fiscal Years 2013 to 2023," Congressional Budget Office, May 2013, http://www.cbo.gov/sites/default/files/cbofiles/attachments/44172-Baseline2.pdf. "Baseline Economic Forecast," Congressional Budget Office, February 2013, http://www.cbo.gov/publication/43902.
92 "History," Centers for Medicare and Medicaid Services, June 13, 2013, http://www.cms.gov/About-CMS/Agency-Information/History/index.html?redirect=/history/; "Medicare Program – General Information," Centers for Medicare and Medicaid Services, August 27, 2013, http://www.cms.gov/Medicare/Medicare-General-Information/MedicareGenInfo/index.html.
93 "Eligibility," Medicaid.gov, accessed September 1, 2013, http://www.medicaid.gov/Medicaid-CHIP-Program-Information/By-Topics/Eligibility/Eligibility.html.
94 "Medicaid Benefits," Medicaid.gov, accessed September 1, 2013, http://www.medicaid.gov/Medicaid-CHIP-Program-Information/By-Topics/Benefits/Medicaid-Benefits.html.

programs, some reducing and some increasing costs. In addition, President Obama's, the Senate Democrats', and the House Republicans' budgets all contain some combination of cost-cutting measures and revenue increases to increase their sustainability.

"Bending The Cost Curve": A Work in Progress

High and rising health care costs explain much of Medicare and Medicaid's budgetary challenges; therefore, controlling overall health care cost growth in the economy remains at the center of federal health policy. In recent decades, the well-documented retirement of the baby-boom generation, longer life spans and a growing demand for health care has increased Medicare expenses substantially.

In 2011, 17.9 percent of total U.S. economic output went toward health care expenditures. This rate has risen steadily for decades, meaning health care costs have grown faster than the overall economy. That said, there is some good news. Since 2003, the rate of growth has actually slowed. For instance, 2011 marked the first year since the economic boom of the 1990s in which health care costs grew at the same pace as GDP. Indeed, since 2009, health care costs have grown by 3.9 percent per year, compared to 9.7 percent in 2002 and 11 percent in 1990.[95] As a result, average annual Medicare cost growth fell from 7.1 percent between 2000 and 2005 to 3.8 percent between 2007 and 2010.[96] Similarly, Medicaid spending fell as a share of GDP from 1.7 percent in 2009 to 1.6 percent in 2012.[97] This trend holds some promise for Medicare and Medicaid sustainability.

Experts disagree on the reason for the slow down. Some believe the reduction is structural; however, others argue that it results from a lower demand for health care services due to the Great Recession of 2008. One recent study attributed 37 percent of the slowdown to the recession, 5 percent to Medicare payment reforms (discussed below), and 55 percent to fundamental changes in the way health care services are delivered and consumed. These changes include slower technological and pharmaceutical innovation, increased cost sharing between patients and insurers, and greater efficiency on the part of hospitals and doctors. These studies indicate lower cost growth in future years.[98] Henry Aaron, health care expert at the Brookings Institution, echoed this analysis in an interview with ARUSA: "If you put all of these factors together, it looks like there's going to be an inflection in the cost curve growth."[99]

Should this low-growth trend continue, the financial states of Medicare and Medicaid would improve markedly. For instance, the President's Council of Economic Advisors estimated in March 2013 that continued 3.6 percent annual cost growth, the rate in recent years, would bring Medicare to only 3.8 percent of GDP by 2085—as opposed to 7 percent under the Medicare Trustees' current forecast.[100] Over the 2013-2022 period alone, overall public sector health care spending would fall by $770 billion.[101]

95 "Historical National Health Expenditure Data," Centers for Medicare and Medicaid Services, January 9, 2013, http://www.cms.gov/Research-Statistics-Data-and-Systems/Statistics-Trends-and-Reports/NationalHealthExpendData/NationalHealthAccountsHistorical.html.

96 Michael Levine and Melinda Buntin, "Why Has Growth in Spending for Fee-For-Service Medicare Slowed?" Congressional Budget Office, August 2013, http://www.cbo.gov/sites/default/files/cbofiles/attachments/44513_MedicareSpendingGrowth-8-22.pdf.

97 "Historical Budget Data."

98 David M. Cutler and Nikhil R. Sahni, "If Slow Rate of Health Care Spending Growth Persists, Projections May Be Off By $770 Billion," *Health Affairs*, May 2013, http://content.healthaffairs.org/content/32/5/841.full.pdf+html?sid=e67360dd-02c6-403d-902a-5d696d2eae48.

99 Henry Aaron, interview by author, August 26, 2013.

100 "Reducing Costs and Improving the Quality of Health Care," 2013 Economic Report of the President, White House Council of Economic Advisors, http://www.whitehouse.gov/sites/default/files/docs/erp2013/ERP2013_Chapter_5.pdf.

101 Cutler and Sahni.

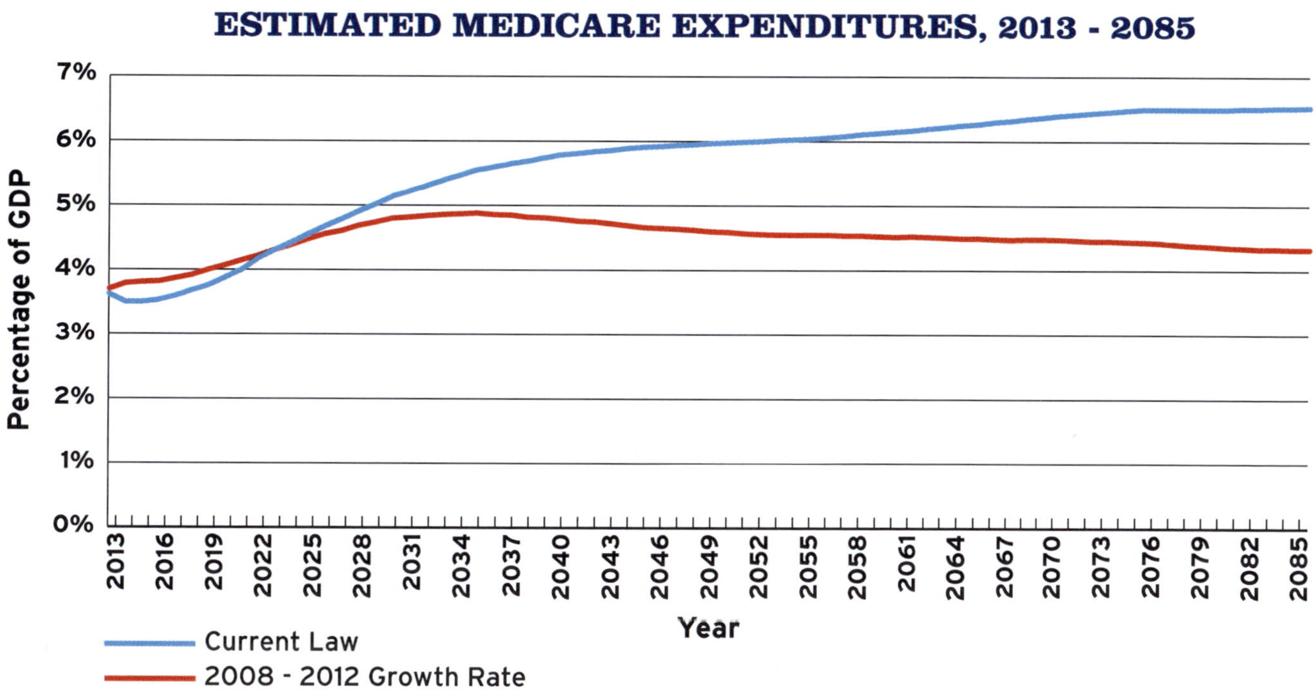

FIGURE 20 SOURCE: Board of Trustees, Federal Hospital Insurance and Federal Supplementary Medical Insurance Trust Funds, http://downloads.cms.gov/files/TR2013.pdf.

In other words, the health care cost growth slowdown could cut the 10-year federal deficit by 10 percent without any further legislation.[102] It should come as no surprise, then, that health care experts and policymakers closely watch the health care cost trend.

Medicare Reform: More to Come?

Recent Reforms

Recent cost trends notwithstanding, Medicare reform lies near the top of many deficit reduction agendas. The Affordable Care Act included $716 billion in cuts to Medicare costs over 10 years.[103] Republicans in the House of Representatives have passed a major overhaul of the program three years in a row as part of Rep. Paul Ryan's budget.[104] President Obama's 2014 budget proposal includes an additional $400 billion in cuts.[105] And while the Senate Democrats did not propose further cuts in 2014, they endorsed the cuts made in the ACA.[106]

An aging population means higher Medicare costs; in fact, the Medicare Trustees expect Medicare's Hospital Insurance Trust Fund to run out in 2026. However, these projections may change if health care costs continue on their slower cost trend of late. If the trust fund does go belly up, hospital insurance benefits will be cut by 13

102 "Updated Budget Projections."
103 "Letter to the Honorable John Boehner," Congressional Budget Office, July 24, 2012, http://www.cbo.gov/sites/default/files/cbofiles/attachments/43471-hr6079.pdf.
104 Paul Ryan, "The Path to Prosperity: A Blueprint for American Renewal," House Budget Committee, March 20, 2012, http://budget.house.gov/uploadedfiles/pathtoprosperity2013.pdf.
105 "Reducing the Deficit in a Smart and Balanced Way," Office of Management and Budget, April 2013, http://www.whitehouse.gov/sites/default/files/omb/budget/fy2014/assets/reducing.pdf.
106 Patty Murray, "Foundation for Growth: Restoring the Promise of American Opportunity," Senate Budget Committee, March 23, 2013, http://www.budget.senate.gov/democratic/index.cfm/files/serve?File_id=c951a802-7600-4111-97c9-20bccc9c69d8.

percent, although doctor and drug benefits would continue in full.[107] Given Medicare's popularity, politicians have good reason to seek reform.

Yet that same popularity poses obstacles to any reform effort. Seventy-two percent of Americans favor the current program, including 88 percent of seniors. Sixty-one percent believe Medicare should provide greater benefits, while between 10 and 36 percent support major spending reductions to aid in deficit reduction.[108] In fact, in August 2013, only 22 percent believed the ACA reforms would improve Medicare, compared to 36 percent who thought they would make the program worse off.[109] These numbers help to explain why Mitt Romney attacked Obama for the ACA cuts, even though they had no effect on beneficiaries—and even though Ryan's budget included the very same cuts.[110] Needless to say, Medicare reform remains one of the biggest political lifts for deficit hawks.

PUBLIC OPINION ON MAJOR MEDICARE SPENDING REDUCTIONS TO REDUCE FEDERAL DEFICIT, 2013

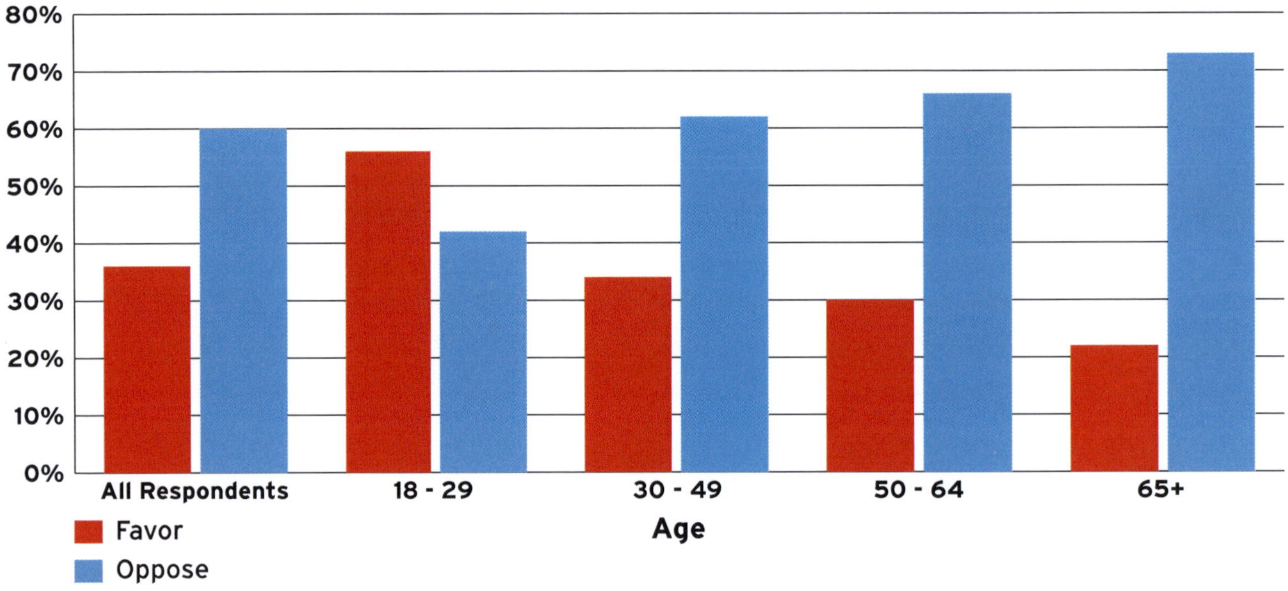

FIGURE 21 SOURCE: New England Journal of Medicine, http://www.nejm.org/doi/full/10.1056/NEJMsr1307622.

107 "2013 Annual Report of the Board of Trustees of the Federal Hospital Insurance and Federal Supplementary Medical Insurance Trust Funds," The Board of Trustees, Federal Hospital Insurance and Federal Supplementary Medical Insurance Trust Funds, May 31, 2013, http://downloads.cms.gov/files/TR2013.pdf.

108 Robert J. Blendon and John M. Benson, "The Public and the Conflict over Future Medicare Spending," *New England Journal of Medicine*, September 12, 2013, http://www.nejm.org/doi/full/10.1056/NEJMsr1307622.

109 "Health Policy," PollingReport.com, accessed September 1, 2013, http://www.pollingreport.com/health.htm.

110 Sarah Kliff, "Romney's Right: Obamacare cuts Medicare by $716 Billion. Here's How," The *Washington Post*, August 14, 2012, http://www.washingtonpost.com/blogs/wonkblog/wp/2012/08/14/romneys-right-obamacare-cuts-medicare-by-716-billion-heres-how/.

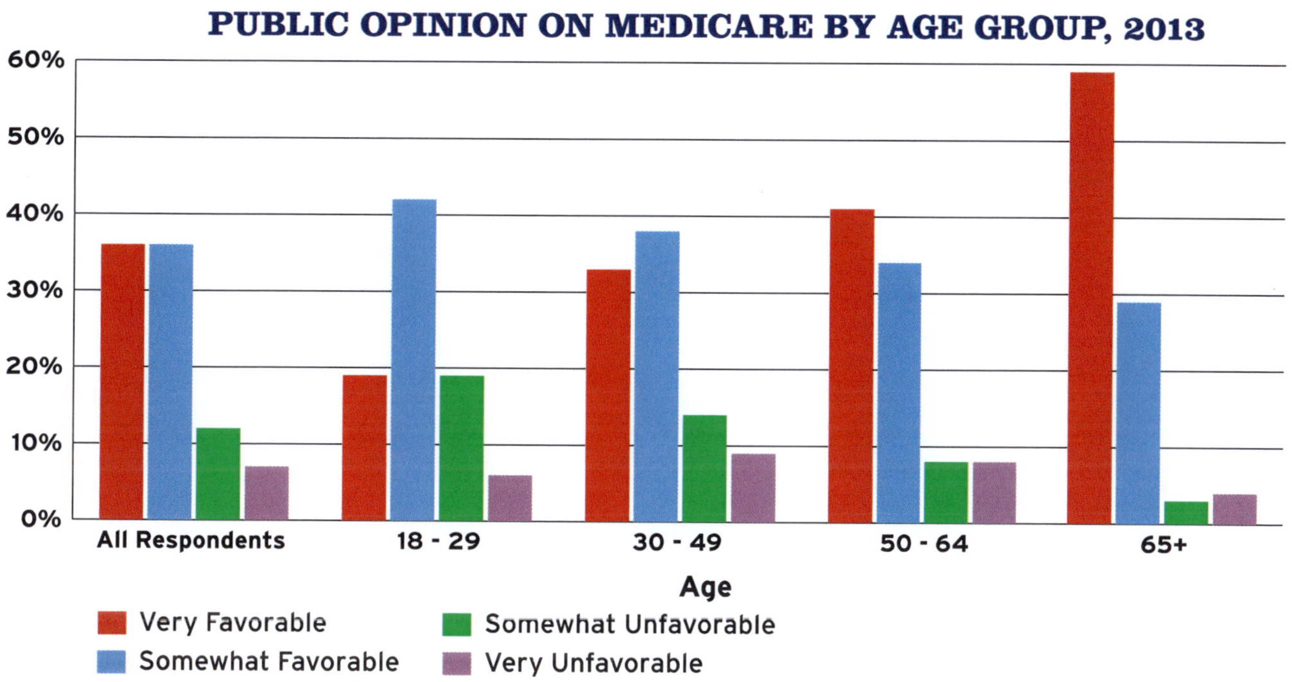

FIGURE 22 SOURCE: New England Journal of Medicine, http://www.nejm.org/doi/full/10.1056/NEJMsr1307622.

Proposed Reforms

In 2013, Democrats and Republicans came no closer to a Medicare reform deal than they have in recent history. The House Republicans budget, passed in March, again proposed changing Medicare's guaranteed benefit into a "premium support" system. Rather than the government paying health providers directly, the plan would provide seniors with a predetermined sum with which to buy private insurance in an exchange. It would also retain the traditional system as an option. Republicans claimed competition among insurers would drive prices down. In addition, the premium support sum would not be allowed to grow beyond GDP growth plus 0.5 percent per year. Finally, the plan would raise the Medicare eligibility age to 67 by 2035. Due to these and other changes, according to the Ryan budget, Medicare costs would fall by $129 billion over 10 years compared to current projections.[111]

The President's 2014 Budget proposed $371 billion in Medicare spending reductions over the next 10 years, albeit in a very different way. Obama's plan combined a patchwork of greater cost sharing by new beneficiaries, higher premiums for the wealthy, and additional cuts to providers on top of ACA cuts to achieve this deficit reduction. Notably, Obama did not include his earlier proposal to increase the eligibility age, likely in response to opposition by congressional Democrats.[112]

While both proposals had their detractors, Republicans' premium support plan was particularly controversial. Democrats and many experts criticized the plan, as they had in previous years, for shifting costs onto seniors and undermining the traditional Medicare system. Many cite the CBO's 2012 predictions that, by 2050, seniors

111 Paul Ryan, "The Path to Prosperity; A Responsible, Balanced Budget," House Budget Committee, March 20, 2013, http://budget.house.gov/uploadedfiles/summary_tablesfy14.pdf.

112 Mary Agnes Carey," "Five Ways the President's Budget Would Change Medicare," Kaiser Health News, April 15, 2013, http://www.kaiserhealthnews.org/stories/2013/april/15/medicare-and-obama-budget.aspx.

would receive up to 42 percent less in Medicare benefits than under the current system. At that point, experts such as Paul Van de Water at the Center for Budget and Policy Priorities claim, many would struggle to afford private insurance. Further, Van de Water and others have claimed that the traditional Medicare program would serve as a fallback for those too sick to receive affordable insurance in the private market, making the system unsustainable.[113] Obama summed up these charges in his 2012 campaign by saying, simply, "No American should ever spend their golden years at the mercy of insurance companies."[114]

For the most part, Republicans responded to the president's 2014 budget offer with a combination of apathy and perfunctory opposition, although some, like Senate Minority Leader Mitch McConnell applauded Obama for wading into entitlement reform.[115] The two sides remain far apart on the Medicare question, even as both hope to claim the mantle of at once protecting and reforming the popular program. According to Aaron, incremental solutions to improve benefits and increase cost sharing for upper incomes could be accomplished "if we weren't in this horrible political environment."[116] "But I don't think it's going to happen anytime soon," he added.[117]

Medicaid Reform: Expand or Contract?

Medicaid stands out from Medicare and Social Security, the two other major entitlement programs, because despite fervent Republican opposition, the program will soon be a lot bigger. The Affordable Care Act expanded Medicaid eligibility to all Americans under 65 who earn up to 133 percent of the poverty line, compared to a median of 48 percent of the poverty line under current state programs.[118] Due to a 2012 Supreme Court ruling that deemed the expansion optional for states, as of September 2013 only 25 states were set to move forward with the expansion on January 1, 2014. Twenty-two states remained opposed.[119] Even with the opposition, an increase of at least 13 million beneficiaries and $710 billion in federal spending is predicted between 2014 and 2023.[120]

This expansion was a big win for Democrats and an instrumental part of their goal to increase health care coverage. Thus, neither President Obama's nor the Senate Democrats' 2014 budget includes changes to Medicaid that go beyond tinkering around the edges. House Republicans, on the other hand, have once again proposed repealing the Medicaid expansion—and all ACA programs, for that matter—and transforming the program from a federal-state cost share to a block grant fully facilitated by the states. The reforms, which Obama rejected, would cut over $800 billion in federal spending over 10 years, or one-third of the total program cost.[121]

The Republican plan to reduce Medicaid spending is simple: give states a predetermined sum to spend on their Medicaid program, give them maximum flexibility, and increase the grant slowly. Ryan and others cite the 1990s welfare reform efforts to show that state flexibility through these "block grants" can slow federal spending significantly. However, critics at the Kaiser Family Foundation and the Center for Budget and Policy Priorities,

113 Paul N. Van de Water, "Medicare in Ryan's 2014 Budget," Center on Budget and Policy Priorities, March 15, 2013, http://www.cbpp.org/cms/?fa=view&id=3922.

114 Mark Landler and Richard A. Oppel, "Obama and Ryan Trade Blasts over Medicare at AARP Convention," *New York Times*, September 21, 2012, http://www.nytimes.com/2012/09/22/us/politics/medicare-takes-center-stage-on-the-campaign-trail.html.

115 John Shaw, "US Budget" Obama Paln Gives Fiscal Debate Energy and Confusion," *MNI News*, April 12, 2013, https://mninews.marketnews.com/index.php/us-budget-obama-plan-gives-fiscal-debate-energy-and-confusion?q=content/us-budget-obama-plan-gives-fiscal-debate-energy-and-confusion.

116 Henry Aaron, interview by author, August 26, 2013.

117 Ibid.

118 "Analyzing the Impact of State Medicaid Expansion Decisions," Kaiser Family Foundation, July 2013, http://kff.org/medicaid/issue-brief/analyzing-the-impact-of-state-medicaid-expansion-decisions/.

119 "Status of State Action on the Medicaid Expansion Decision, as of September 20, 2013," Kaiser Family Foundation, September 30, 2013, http://kff.org/health-reform/state-indicator/state-activity-around-expanding-medicaid-under-the-affordable-care-act/#map.

120 "Effects of Affordable Care Act on Health Insurance Coverage," Congressional Budget Office, May 2013, http://www.cbo.gov/sites/default/files/cbofiles/attachments/43900-2013-05-ACA.pdf.

121 Paul Ryan, "The Path to Prosperity; A Responsible, Balanced Budget," House Budget Committee, March 20, 2013, http://budget.house.gov/uploadedfiles/fy14budget.pdf.

among others, have noted that these grants would not keep pace with expected Medicaid costs and would lead states to kick off beneficiaries from their rolls. This discrepancy would prove acute in recessions, when state budgets struggle just as poverty rates increase.[122] Indeed, opponents see the plan much like they see Ryan's Medicare reforms, both of which they claim achieve savings only by shifting costs to states and individuals.

HOUSE REPUBLICAN MEDICARE CUTS AS PERCENTAGE OF CURRENT LAW, 2013 - 2022

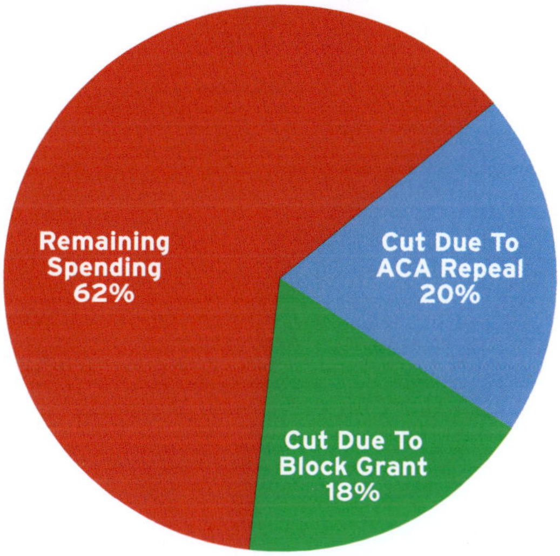

FIGURE 23 SOURCE: Kaiser Family Foundation , http://kaiserfamilyfoundation.files.wordpress.com/2013/01/8185-02.pdf.

HOUSE REPUBLICAN MEDICARE CUTS AS PERCENTAGE OF CURRENT LAW, 2022

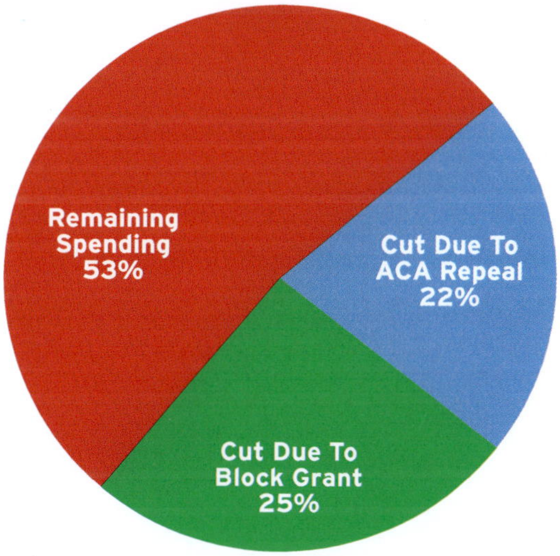

FIGURE 24 SOURCE: Kaiser Family Foundation , http://kaiserfamilyfoundation.files.wordpress.com/2013/01/8185-02.pdf.

122 Edwin Park and Matt Broaddus, "Ryan Block Grant Proposal Would Cut Medicaid by Nearly One-Third by 2023 and More After That," Center on Budget and Policy Priorities, March 26, 2013, http://www.cbpp.org/cms/?fa=view&id=3941; "Implications of a Federal Block Grant for Medicaid," Kaiser Family Foundation, April 2011, http://kaiserfamilyfoundation.files.wordpress.com/2013/01/8173.pdf.

Barring an unexpected deal between President Obama and Congressional Republicans, Medicaid expansion will continue apace, and the program will grow into the future.

Watching Closely

For the present, major reforms to contain costs in either Medicaid or Medicare have little chance of passing in today's fraught political environment. Yet signs of a structural change in health care costs and an expansion in Medicaid enacted into law three years ago mean both Medicare and Medicaid will see major shifts regardless of further legislative action. Policymakers will surely watch both of these processes closely to assess the budgetary effects of these programs and the most feasible paths for reform when it becomes necessary.

★

FOREIGN RELATIONS AND SECURITY: Defense

by Priyanka Menon

Defense spending has always been a high-profile issue, especially in times of economic hardship such as the years following the Great Recession. The sequester has left the Department of Defense (DOD) reeling from budget cuts, with mandatory furloughs and reductions in acquisitions, benefits, and health care being put in place. In light of the Budget Control Act of 2011, the size and form of the DOD's budget has been subject to much discussion among military officials, lawmakers, and civilians. Much effort has been paid to reshaping the DOD as a whole to be better equipped to meet the military threats of the 21st century, which veer from traditional forms.

Effects of the Sequester

The Department of Defense has not been immune from the effects of sequestration. As a result of the FY 2013 cuts, the Department of Defense saw a $37 billion decrease in funding. The Budget Control Act, the legislation responsible for sequestration, mandated that all DOD budget accounts be reduced by 10 percent, excepting military personnel accounts. On the ground level, these budgets cuts translated into truncated training periods and furloughs for DOD employees.[123] As a result of the furloughs, 85 percent of all Pentagon employees were mandated to take six days of unpaid leave, impacting DOD productivity and functionality.[124]

Sequestration also impacted the acquisition of new weapons and technology by the military. The Air Force, Navy, and Marine Corps all saw budget reductions impact the amount and type of weapons they could acquire. Chief of Naval Operations Admiral Jonathan W. Greenert stated these costs impacted the readiness of the armed forces and it could take the Navy several years to recover from the effects of sequestration.[125] [126] In FY 2013, the Navy saw an $11 billion budget reduction.[127] Additionally, sequestration caused a reduction in the amount of funding for defense research. The DOD reduced the amount of money for research as well as the number of scientists and researchers it financed.[128]

Military families were also affected by the DOD budget cuts. Though military pay was protected, TriCare, the military health care system, was cut by $3 billion.[129] Civilians, the DOD employees subject to the majority of DOD furloughs, make up as much as 40 percent of the military health care system. Thus patient care and pharmaceutical efficiency, among other things, suffered. Military schools also suffered; many of the civilian employees at DOD schools were subject to furloughs. However, the major funding cuts to schools located on or near military bases have come as a result of cuts to funding at the Department of Education, specifically to Impact Aid.[130] It is cuts like these that highlight the far-reaching effects of sequestration.

---

123 Marcus Weisgurber, "Sequestration Could Chop $33B from DoD Investments," *Defense News*, July 10, 2013, http://www.defensenews.com/article/20130710/DEFREG02/307100020/Sequestration-Could-Chop-33B-from-DoD-Investments.

124 Tony Capaccio, "Pentagon Releases Report on Sequestration Cuts' Effects," Bloomberg, June 11, 2013, http://www.bloomberg.com/news/2013-06-11/pentagon-releases-report-on-sequestration-cuts-effects.html.

125 "CNO Details Navy's Fiscal 2014 Budget Realities," The Official Website of the United States Navy, Jim Garamone, September 5, 2013, http://www.navy.mil/submit/display.asp?story_id=76359.

126 "DoD officials warn of damaging effects from likely sequestration in FY2014," The American Society of Military Comptrollers, September 6, 2013, http://www.asmconline.org/2013/09/dod-officials-warn-of-damaging-effects-from-likely-sequestration-in-fy2014/.

127 Ibid.

128 Linda Kyzer, "Sequestration Limits Defense Research and Development," ClearanceJobs.com, April 25, 2013, http://news.clearancejobs.com/2013/04/25/sequestration-limits-defense-research-and-development/.

129 "Sequestration: What Does It Mean For Military Families?" National Military Family Association, http://www.militaryfamily.org/feature-articles/sequestration-what-does-it.html.

130 "Budget cuts to hit military school districts first," *USA Today*, March 2, 2013, http://www.usatoday.com/story/news/nation/2013/03/02/budget-cuts-military-schools/1958479/.

FY 2014 Funding Overview

Looking at FY 2014, none in the defense community are too enthused. If sequestration continues, many military officials predict drastic reductions in the readiness and quality of the armed services. Because the funding cuts for FY 2013 have already caused delayed response times, truncated training, and furloughs, military officials claim that the next round of cuts will have even larger effects. These cuts could severely impact the structure of the military, with some sections of the military considering RIFs, reductions-in-forces, as their only option for dealing with renewed cuts.[131]

In an eight page letter to Senators Carl Levin and James Inhofe, chairman and ranking member of the Senate Armed Services Committee, Secretary of Defense Chuck Hagel described the effects of the budget cuts should Congress fail to prevent them from going into place for FY 2014.[132] Military training, size, and technological capacity would be reduced.[133] Furthermore, research and development would be severely hindered, with the Pentagon likely forced to cut close to 20 percent of its budget for procurement and research and development.[134] The sequestration cuts would also continue to make military workers' lives "difficult," as stated by Frank Kendall, undersecretary of defense for acquisition, technology and logistics.[135]

CBO ESTIMATES OF DEPARTMENT OF DEFENSE EXPENDITURES, 2014 - 2022

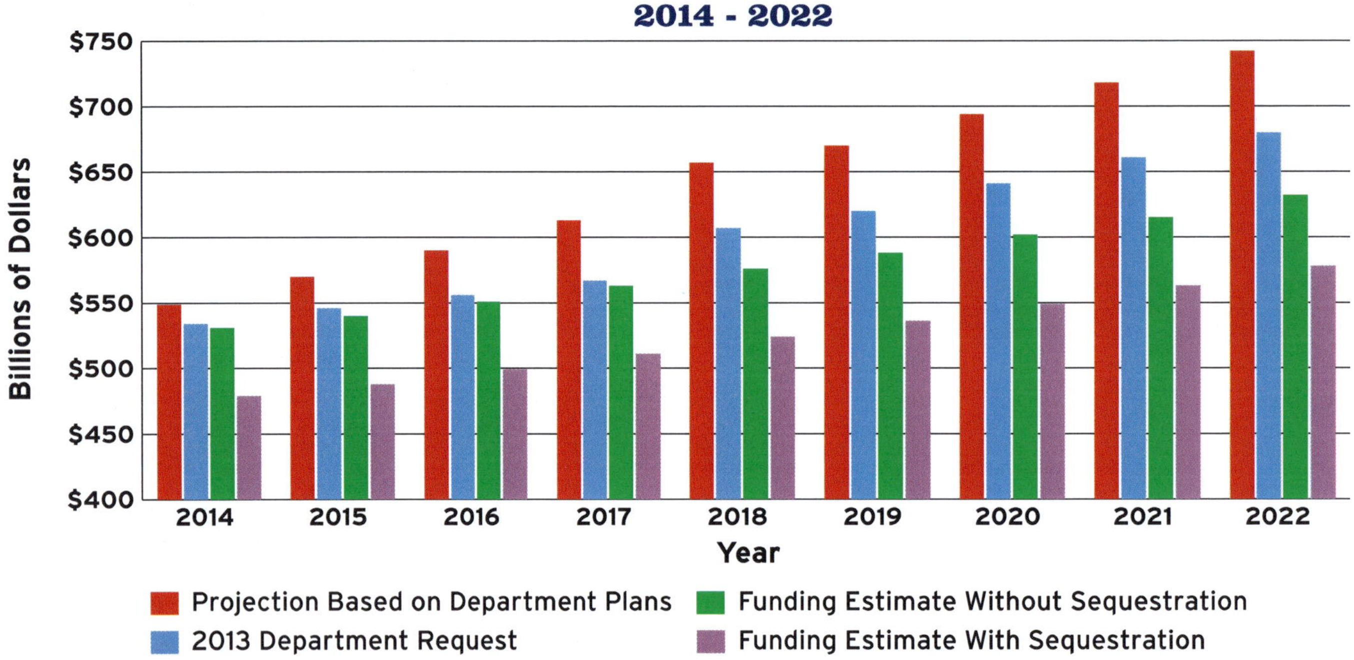

FIGURE 25 SOURCE: Congressional Budget Office, http://www.cbo.gov/sites/default/files/cbofiles/attachments/07-11-12-FYDP_forPosting_0.pdf.

131 Tony Capaccio, "Pentagon Weighs Firing Thousands Under 2014 Spending Cuts," Bloomberg, August 23, 2013, http://www.bloomberg.com/news/2013-08-22/pentagon-weighs-firing-thousands-under-2014-spending-cuts.html.

132 Marcus Weisgurber, "Sequestration Could Chop $33B from DoD Investments," *Defense News*, July 10, 2013, http://www.defensenews.com/article/20130710/DEFREG02/307100020/Sequestration-Could-Chop-33B-from-DoD-Investments.

133 Ibid.

134 ibid.

135 "Official Predicts Bleak Budget Picture for Fiscal 2014," *American Forces Press Service*, September 5, 2013, http://www.defense.gov/news/newsarticle.aspx?id=120726.

The president's FY 2014 budget request, which sidesteps the possibility of continued sequestration and budget cuts to the DOD, includes $526 billion in discretionary funding for the Department of Defense, a $3.9 billion or 0.7 percent decrease from 2012 levels.[136] Among the DOD's priorities for this fiscal year are to "reform the Department's acquisitions processes," "responsibly [draw] down our military presence in Afghanistan," and "[take] steps to control rising health care costs without sacrificing quality of care," in addition to providing for the nation's defense (Figure 26).[137]

The budget also highlights the president's commitment to increasing U.S. presence in the Asia-Pacific region, stating that "DOD and other agencies are devoting greater energy and resources to revitalizing U.S. alliances and economic ties across the Asia-Pacific region."[138] Guam received renewed attention from the president's budget in the form of $95 million for infrastructure, as it is geographically crucial in the president's "pivot to Asia."[139]

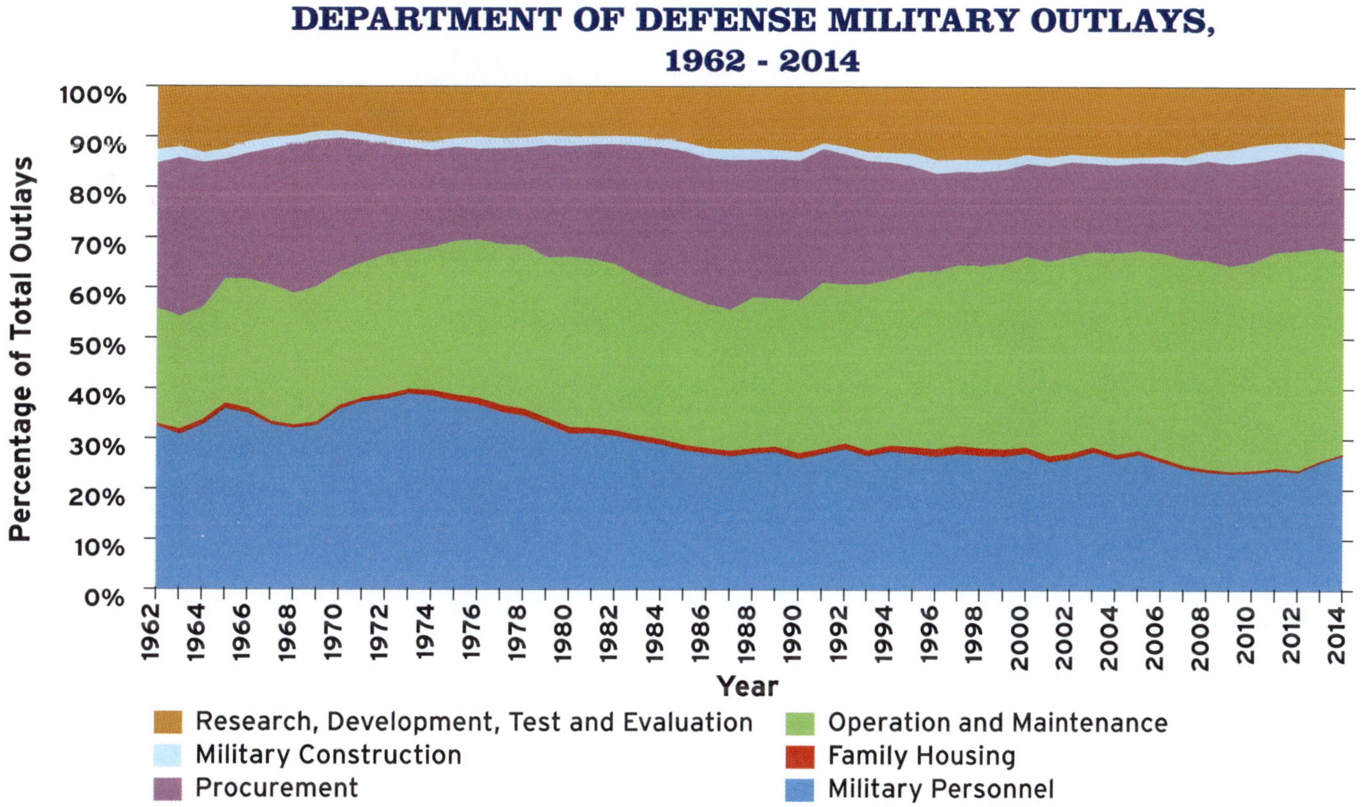

FIGURE 26 SOURCE: Office of Management and Budget, http://www.whitehouse.gov/sites/default/files/omb/budget/fy2014/assets/hist03z2.xls.

The president's budget also increased the amount of DOD attention placed on Cybersecurity and Cyberspace operations. The budget promotes the use of the Cyber Forces of the U.S. Cyber Command, a group of defensive, intelligence, and analytical experts that counter and prevent cyber attacks and conduct reconnaissance on the

136 "Department of Defense Funding Highlights," the White House, http://www.whitehouse.gov/sites/default/files/omb/budget/fy2014/assets/defense.pdf.
137 Ibid.
138 Ibid.
139 Ibid.

development of possible cyber security risks and threats.[140] Also included in the budget is increased funding for cyber information sharing through the Comprehensive National Cybersecurity Initiative Five.[141]

In March of 2013, the Senate approved a $594 billion budget for the DOD, seeking to ameliorate the effects the sequestration cuts have had on the DOD.[142] This includes $78 billion allocated towards the war in Afghanistan, including a special provision that dictates none of the money may go to benefitting Hamid Karzai personally.[143] This portion of the bill is in direct response to claims that Karzai had been using money from the CIA for personal benefit.[144]

The Senate bill also came in $91 billion over the sequester-mandated topline, at $1.085 trillion in defense and non-defense discretionary budget.[145] This $91 billion excess sparked concern among Republican lawmakers, with Senator Lindsey Graham (R-S. Car.) stating, "We screwed ourselves over here," to Washington-based newsmagazine *The Hill*, referring to Congress' decision to ignore the topline sequestration caps.[146]

On the other side of the Capitol, the House passed a similar budget, approving $595 billion in spending for the DOD. The House budget contains similar measures as the Senate bill, with $82.3 billion in war spending as well as provisions for a 1 percent pay increase for military members.[147]

The House discretionary budget came in at the sequestration topline limit, due to large cuts to domestic discretionary spending, including potential cuts to programs such as Meals-on-Wheels, Head Start, and NIH grant funding.[148] In spite of these cuts to domestic programs, the bill does not incorporate cost-cutting measures for the Pentagon, forgoing White House recommended base closures and TriCare fee raises and restoring the Department of Defense's budget to pre-sequester levels.[149] These cuts to domestic programs have sparked claims from the White House that the House spent excessively on defense at the expense of the social safety net.[150] Because of this, the president threatened to veto the House budget,[151] calling for the House and Senate appropriations committees to go to conference to resolve these issues.[152]

Moving Forward from the Sequester

Even if Congress comes to a budgetary consensus and ends the sequester, the issue remains that changes must be made to the budgetary structure of the United States armed forces. In order to maintain the United States' strategic interests and adapt the military to face 21st century security threats, the Pentagon's budget must be restructured. That much is clear.

140 Ibid.
141 Ibid.
142 Richard Lardner, "Senate panel approves 2014 defense spending bill," *Businessweek*, July 30, 2013, http://www.businessweek.com/ap/2013-07-30/senate-panel-approves-2014-defense-spending-bill.
143 Ibid.
144 Ibid.
145 Jeremy Herb, "Senate panel clears $594B Defense appropriations bill," *The Hill*, August 1, 2013, http://thehill.com/blogs/defcon-hill/budget-appropriations/315041-senate-panel-clears-594b-defense-appropriations-bill.
146 Ibid.
147 Ibid.
148 Ibid.
149 Rick Maze, "White House issues veto threat of defense funding bill," *Navy Times*, July 22, 2013, http://www.navytimes.com/article/20130722/NEWS05/307220041/White-House-issues-veto-threat-defense-funding-bill.
150 Ibid.
151 Ibid.
152 Jeremy Herb, "Senate panel clears $594B," *The Hill*, August 1, 2013, http://thehill.com/blogs/defcon-hill/budget-appropriations/315041-senate-panel-clears-594b-defense-appropriations-bill.

How to achieve this, however, is a much murkier issue. The Hamilton Project at the Brookings Institute proposes a three part strategy in Cindy Williams's discussion paper, Making Defense Affordable, that includes designing "a defense force better aligned to face future challenges," improving the "efficiency and efficacy of the acquisitions system," and controlling "rising personnel costs."[153] Specifically, the project advocates redesigning the military's health care system, as "health care is the fastest-growing element of the defense budget," and limiting military pay raises and housing allowances.[154] Ultimately, Williams proposes reducing the size of the U.S. military, though "the U.S. military would still greatly outspend every other military in the world by a sizeable margin."[155]

GLOBAL MILITARY EXPENDITURES, 2012 (billions of dollars)

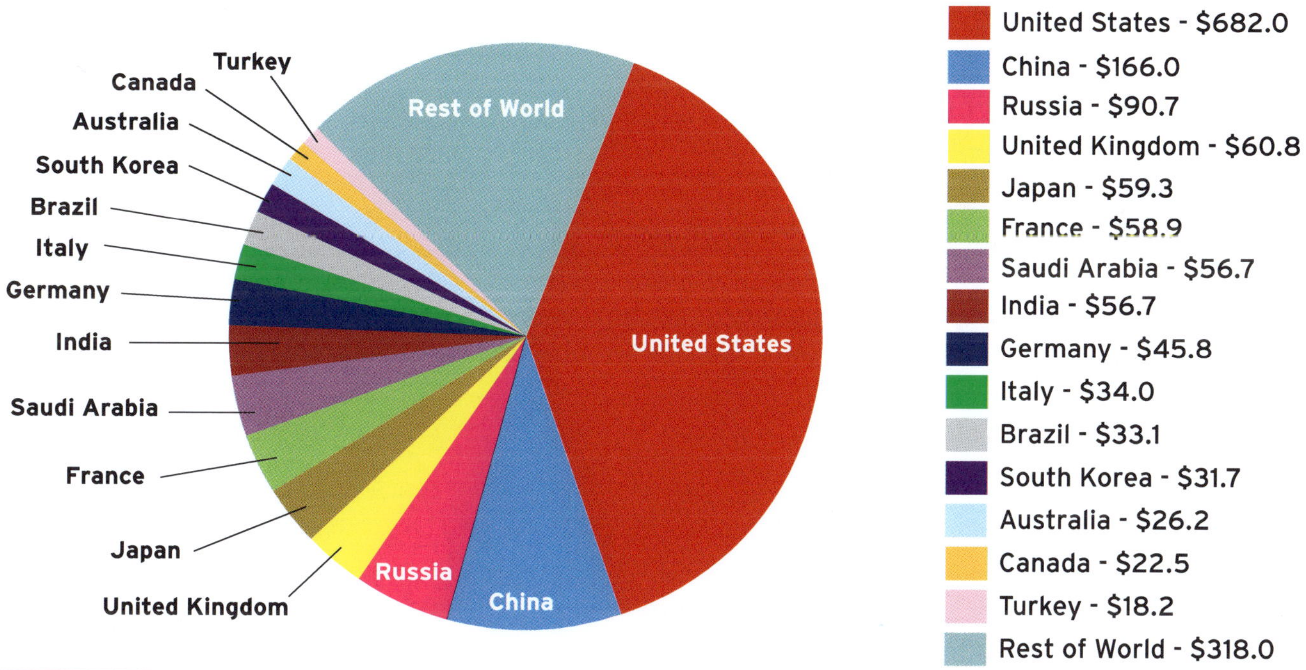

FIGURE 27 SOURCE: Stockholm International Peace Research Institute, http://www.statista.com/statistics/262742/countries-with-the-highest-military-spending/.

Williams goes on to propose changes in the structure of the military, as well as a strategic shift that moves away from the mentality that "sees virtually any conflict around the globe as a vital interest for the United States and that aims to remake the rest of the world in America's image."[156] Moreover, Williams establishes the fact that the stagnation of the allocation of resources within the DOD, a proportion that has not changed since the Cold War, translates into an inefficient military.[157] As an alternative, she presents two options for reshaping defense spending for the future, either by reducing each department's non-war budget or by reallocating resources to increase the United States' presence in the Pacific Asia region.[158]

Richard Betts, a senior fellow at the Council on Foreign Relations, proposed fundamentally rethinking how the Pentagon addresses security and defense issues. He claims that the Cold War era strategy of deterrence has little

153 "National Defense in a Time of Change," The Hamilton Project, February 2013, http://www.brookings.edu/research/papers/2013/02/us-national-defense-changes.
154 Cindy Williams, "Making Defense Affordable," The Hamilton Project, February 2013, http://www.hamiltonproject.org/files/downloads_and_links/THP_WilliamsDiscPaper.pdf.
155 Ibid.
156 Ibid.
157 Ibid.
158 Ibid.

use in the 21st century, harming rather than hurting the United States' defense policy.[159] The United States has invested billions of dollars in developing and acquiring technology and weapons that give it an advantage in a standard war scenario, while its main 21st century enemy, namely Iran, has "never launched a regular war against its enemies."[160]

Looking outside of the Middle East to Asia provides similar arguments against deterrence: China and the United States' "economic interdependence precludes military conflict," says Betts.[161] Thus, simply amassing weapons and technology does little to further U.S. interests; continuing to do so would only place a further strain on the defense budget.

Conclusion

National defense, obviously, is an issue of utmost importance. After all, the preamble to the Constitution makes it imperative that the government of the United States "provide for the common defense."[162] However, over two centuries later, the definition and implications of providing for the common defense have changed drastically, bringing with them ramifications for the future of the nation as a whole. Sequestration has brought to light negative effects of ballooning defense spending, causing many to call for a fundamental rethinking of defense policy in the United States military. How the DOD chooses to respond to these claims could very well set the course of the nation for generations to come.

★

159 Richard Betts, "The Lost Logic of Deterrence," Foreign Affairs, March/April 2013, http://www.foreignaffairs.com/articles/138846/richard-k-betts/the-lost-logic-of-deterrence.
160 Ibid.
161 Ibid.
162 "Preamble," Legal Information Institute, http://www.law.cornell.edu/constitution/preamble.

FOREIGN RELATIONS AND SECURITY: Immigration

by Priyanka Menon

Federal immigration policy, and immigration reform in particular, breaches social and political divides like few other budget issues. Aside from being an existential crisis over America's identity as a nation of immigrants, the debate over immigration reform is also a budgetary one, significantly impacting the economic health and outlook of the United States. However, being an incredibly complex issue, the exact economic effects of immigration reform are unclear, evading most methods of precise economic analysis. As a result, the predictions on the effects of immigration are as varied as they are significant.

BUDGETARY IMPLICATIONS OF S. 744

S.744, or the Border Security, Economic Opportunity, and Immigration Modernization Act, was authored by four Republican and four Democratic senators (known as the "Gang of Eight") in early 2013 as a bipartisan proposal for broad immigration reform, both on the law enforcement and structural policy ends.

Even for the Congressional Budget Office, the far-reaching, lasting effects of immigration reform make a rather unwieldy subject for economic analysis. Sticking to its standard procedure, CBO estimates that the provisions in S. 744 would increase direct federal spending by $298 billion from 2014 to 2023.[163] Much of this would be brought on by increased refundable income tax credits and increased spending on health care-related entitlement programs, a result of the larger legal population.[164]

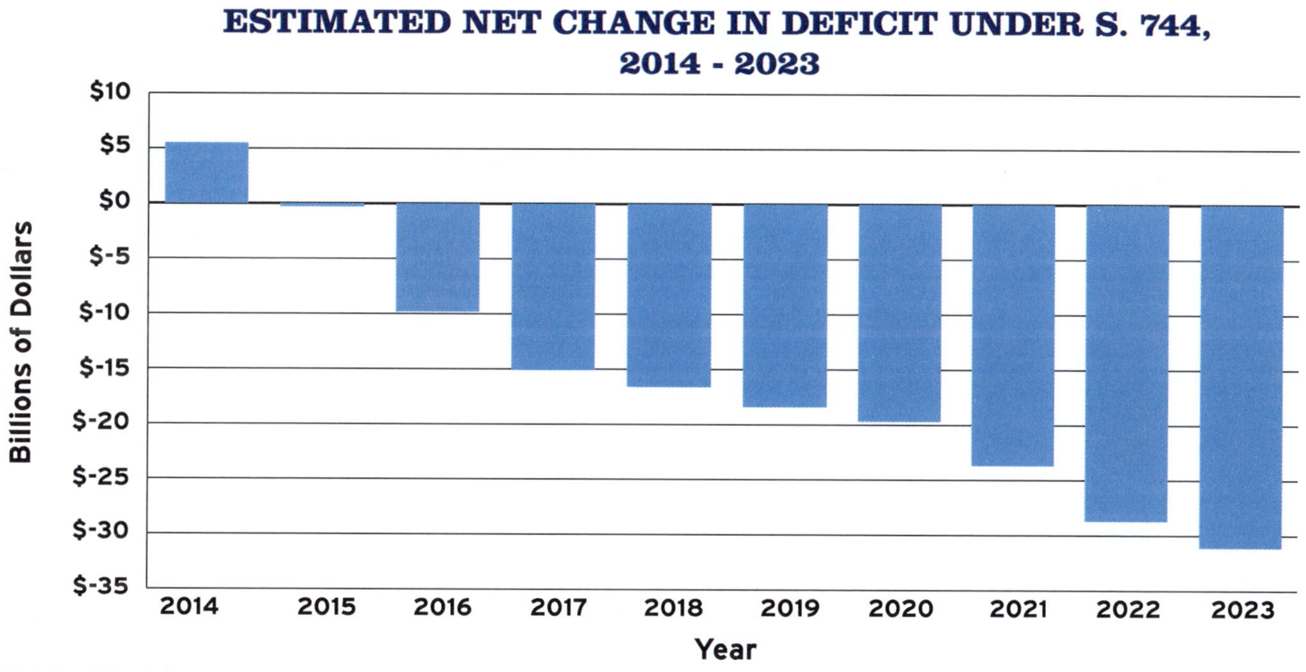

FIGURE 28 SOURCE: Congressional Budget Office, http://www.cbo.gov/sites/default/files/cbofiles/attachments/s744aspassed.pdf.

163 Congressional Budget Office, July 2013, http://www.cbo.gov/sites/default/files/cbofiles/attachments/s744aspassed.pdf.
164 Congressional Budget Office, July 2013, http://www.cbo.gov/sites/default/files/cbofiles/attachments/s744aspassed.pdf.

The bill also allocated $46.3 billion toward increased border protection efforts in order to implement expanded border security measures and ameliorate the costs of processing an increased number of visa applications.[165]

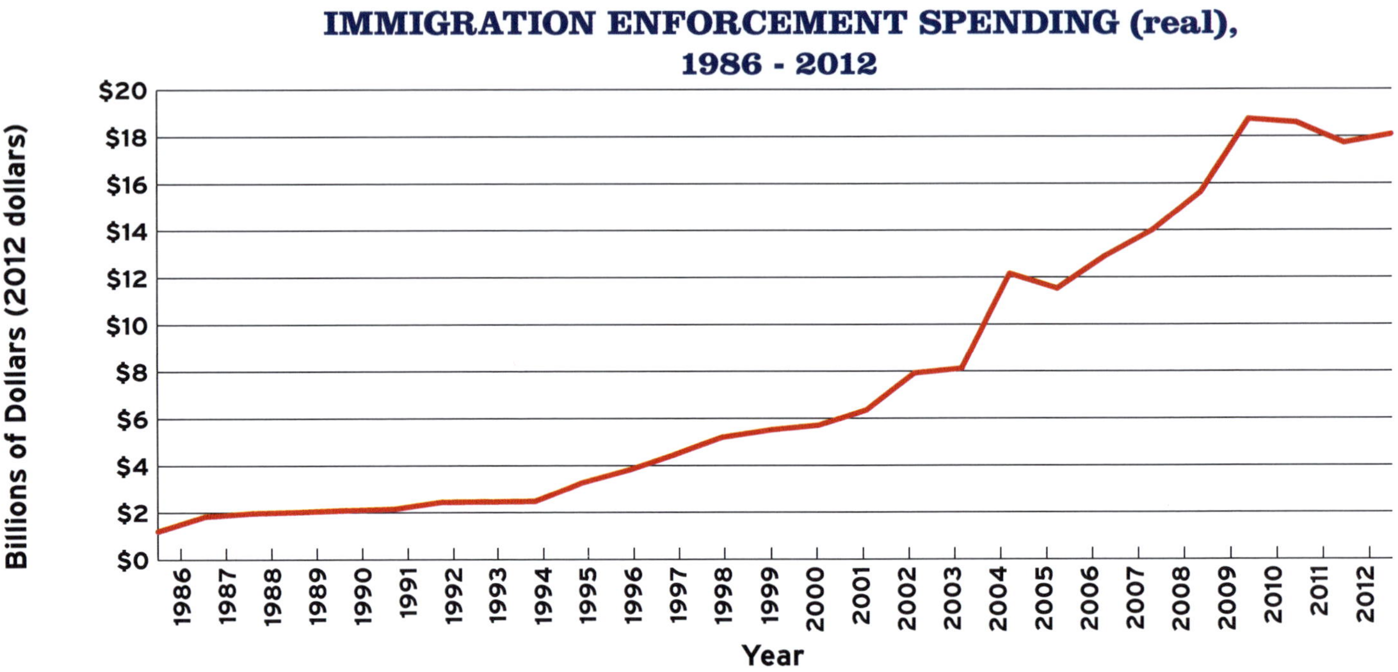

FIGURE 29

SOURCE: U.S. Department of Homeland Security and U.S. Department of Justice, http://www.dhs.gov/dhs-budget and http://www.justice.gov/archive/jmd/1975_2002/2002/html/page104-108.htm.

1986 - 2003 data represent Immigration and Naturalization Service budget under Department of Justice.

2004 - 2012 data represent combined budgets of US Customs and Border Protection, US Immigration and Customs Enforcement, and the US Visitor and Immigrant Status Indicator Technology under the Department of Homeland Security.

Among expanded measures include a two-fold increase in the number of border patrol agents and aerial drone surveillance of the border.[166] As a result, CBO estimates that S. 744, in conjunction with the Corker-Hoeven amendment, a last-minute addition to the bill that increased border security funding in order to get greater conservative support for reform, would reduce illegal immigration to the United States by one-half to two-thirds of current levels.[167] On the whole, the cost of implementing S. 744 would result in an increase of $23 billion in discretionary spending from 2014-2023.[168] The agency further estimates a higher level of revenue from federal income and payroll taxes, resulting in an increase in federal revenue of $456 billion during the same period. Because of the structural changes in federal spending and taxation brought on by the bill, CBO estimates a decrease of $158 billion in the federal budget deficit over the decade.[169]

However, as a consequence of CBO practices established in 1974, these estimates fail to incorporate the changes in macroeconomic values, such as GDP, caused by S. 744.[170] Because the actual size of these values tend to be

165 Congressional Budget Office, July 2013, http://www.cbo.gov/sites/default/files/cbofiles/attachments/s744aspassed.pdf.
166 Brad Plumer, "CBO: Senate immigration bill now cuts illegal immigration by half," *Washington Post*, July 3, 2013, http://www.washingtonpost.com/blogs/wonkblog/wp/2013/07/03/cbo-senate-immigration-bill-now-cuts-illegal-immigration-by-half/.
167 Ibid.
168 "S. 744, Border Security, Economic Opportunity, and Immigration Modernization Act," Congressional Budget Office, July 3, 2013, http://www.cbo.gov/publication/44397.
169 Congressional Budget Office, July 2013, http://www.cbo.gov/sites/default/files/cbofiles/attachments/s744aspassed.pdf.
170 "The Economic Impact of S. 744, the Border Security, Economic Opportunity, and Immigration Modernization Act," Congressional Budget Office, June 2013, http://www.cbo.gov/sites/default/files/cbofiles/attachments/44346-Immigration.pdf.

disputed within the economist community, CBO avoids taking into account these macroeconomic factors so as to prevent any disputes over the credibility and neutrality of their reports. Additionally, the initial CBO figures discount the influence of S. 744 on economic factors such as labor growth, productivity, rate of return, and income earned by capital; CBO does report its calculated estimates for these figures, though it publishes them in a separate report.[171] In these cost estimates, though CBO acknowledges the uncertainty of its claims, it states point-blank, "S. 744 would boost economic output."[172] In its projections, CBO estimates a 3.3 percent increase in GDP by 2023 and a 5.4 increase ten years later.[173] Furthermore, though S. 744 would result in decreased average wages for the first twelve years after its passage, it would cause an increase in the average wage in the United States from 2025 onwards.[174] Overall, CBO found that S. 744 would result in increased productivity for labor and capital, higher levels of capital investment, higher unemployment rates through 2020, and raised interest rates.

ESTIMATED CHANGES IN DIRECT SPENDING AND REVENUES UNDER S. 744, 2014 - 2023

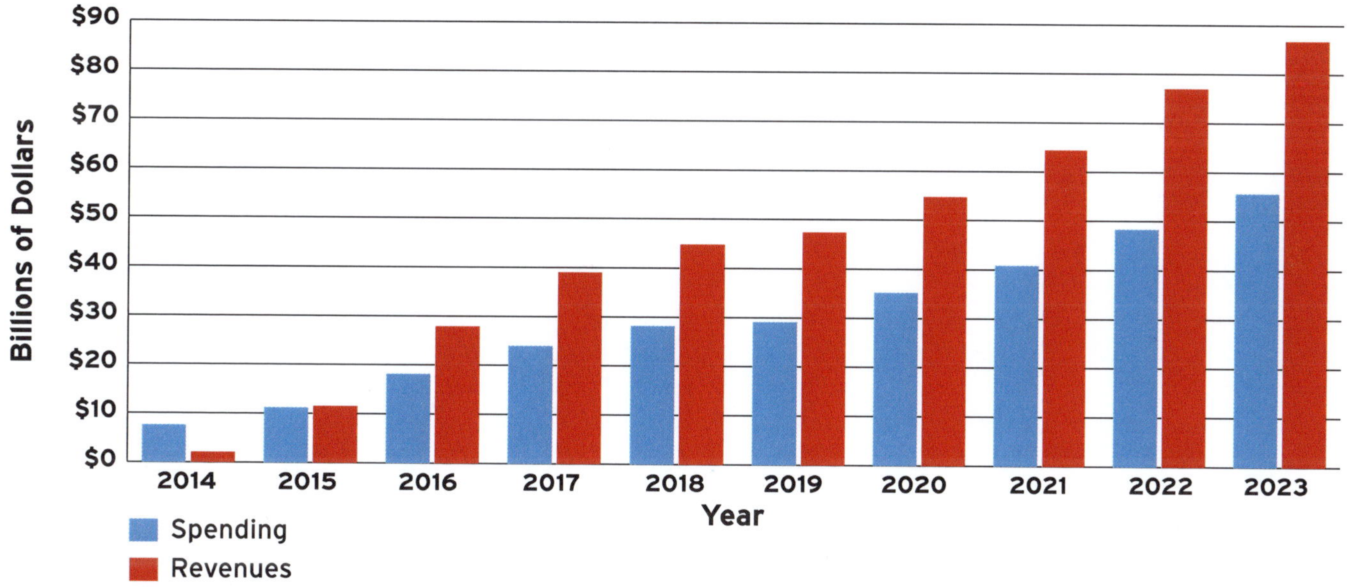

FIGURE 30 SOURCE: Congressional Budget Office, http://www.cbo.gov/sites/default/files/cbofiles/attachments/s744aspassed.pdf.

PERSPECTIVES FROM BOTH SIDES OF THE AISLE

Clearly, immigration reform is a complex issue that evades simple analysis. However, one can better illuminate the complexity of the issue by looking various stances of think tanks on the issue. While the Cato Institute, the Center for American Progress, and the American Action Forum, a group of strange bedfellows to say the least, all agree that immigration reform would reduce the deficit, the Heritage Foundation and Center for Immigration Studies maintain that it would increase it.[175] Entering the fray is the OECD (Organization for Economic Cooperation and Development), which argues that immigration reform would not shift the deficit significantly in either direction.

171 Ibid.
172 "The Economic Impact of S. 744, the Border Security, Economic Opportunity, and Immigration Modernization Act," Congressional Budget Office, June 18, 2013, http://www.cbo.gov/publication/44346.
173 Ibid.
174 Ibid.
175 Annie Lowery, "Immigration and Fiscal Policy," *New York Times*, August 8, 2013, http://economix.blogs.nytimes.com/2013/06/26/immigration-and-fiscal-policy/?_r=0.

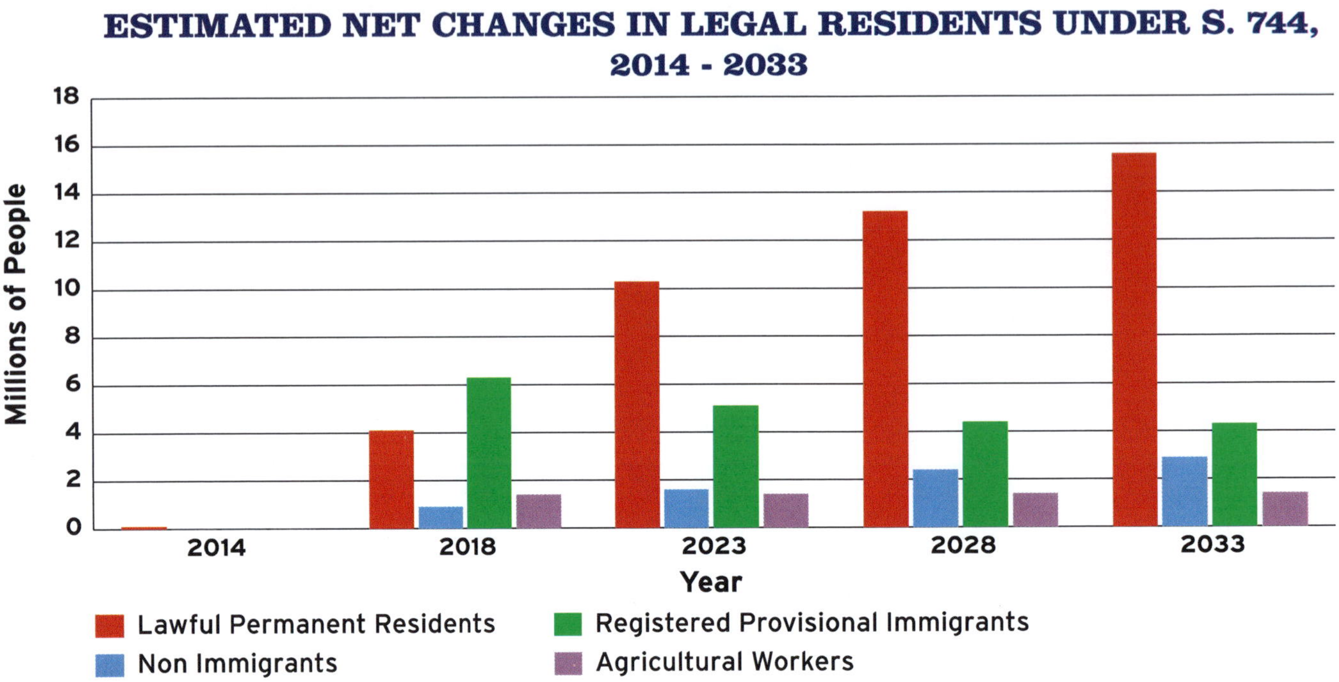

FIGURE 31 SOURCE: Congressional Budget Office, http://cbo.gov/sites/default/files/cbofiles/attachments/s744.pdf.

In looking at the analysis completed by the American Action Forum, a conservative think tank, one finds that in addition to considering the effect increased population growth will have on GDP, the paper also accounts for the "entrepreneurial bent" of immigrants.[176] Though this is a rather unorthodox variable to include in an economic analysis, the AAF's report does so, in the form of increased output and productivity per worker.[177] The report also notes that immigrant women have higher fertility rates than native women, leading to increase population growth.[178] In turn, this causes greater GDP growth, productivity growth, and ultimately, a higher standard of living, or GDP per capita.[179] Much of this analysis hangs on the assumption that "innovation is at least in part embodied into the quality of consumer," as well as the previously noted observation concerning birth rates among immigrant and native women.[180]

In contrast, the liberal Center for American Progress's analysis of the issues largely avoids this attempt to quantify these nontraditional factors. Instead, CAP's report presents numbers such as prospective GDP growth rate if immigration reform had gone into effect in 2009 and the amount of tax revenue the federal government would gain if all undocumented immigrants were given legal status.[181] However, a second glance at CAP's inclusion of figures such as "revenue generated by immigrants," in which it presents the amount of tax revenue generated by Fortune 500 companies founded by immigrants or first generation Americans, proves that CAP's report too contains some unorthodox economic figuring.[182] These numbers, though perhaps more seemingly quantitative than

176 Douglas Holtz-Eakin, "Immigration and the Economy and the Budget," American Action Forum, April 2013, http://americanactionforum.org/sites/default/files/Immigration%20and%20the%20Economy%20and%20Budget.pdf.
177 Ibid.
178 Ibid.
179 Ibid.
180 Ibid.
181 Angela Maria Kelley and Philip E. Wolgin, "10 Reason Why Immigration Reform is Important to Our Fiscal Health," Center for American Progress, September 29, 2011, http://www.americanprogress.org/issues/immigration/news/2011/09/29/10375/10-reasons-why-immigration-reform-is-important-to-our-fiscal-health/.
182 Ibid.

the American Action Forum's arithmetic surrounding the entrepreneurial bent of immigrants, aim to quantify the potential entrepreneurial spirit of the newly legalized immigrants under immigration reform, another element that evades orthodox quantification.

As previously mentioned, the Cato Institute report, though aimed at responding to Congress's and the Bush administration's 2006 attempt at comprehensive immigration reform, draws the same conclusions as the American Action Forum's and the Center for American Progress' studies. The study finds that though the low-skilled immigrants may be a fiscal burden to the states and counties they inhabit, they are a fiscal asset to the federal government, causing higher labor productivity and revenue levels.[183] The report goes on to point out the other numerous virtues of immigrants, such as higher fertility rates and a diverse workforce.[184]

TABLE 4 - PROS AND CONS OF REFORM

CATO INSTITUTE	AMERICAN ACTION FORUM	CENTER FOR AMERICAN PROGRESS
✔ Decreases federal budget deficits ✘ Immigrants are a fiscal burden to local and state governments ✔ Immigration results in higher productivity levels, which leads to higher revenue levels	✔ Increased population growth would give rise to increased productivity and thus increase GDP ✔ Higher fertility rates lead to increased population and increased GDP and GDP per capita	✔ Increases government tax revenues ✔ Increases population growth, and thus GDP
HERITAGE FOUNDATION	**CENTER FOR IMMIGRATION STUDIES**	**ORGANIZATION FOR ECONOMIC CO-OPERATION AND DEVELOPMENT**
✘ Increases government-sponsored services and benefits ✘ Government spending would increase, offsetting any tax revenue gained from legalizing immigrant populations	✘ The cost of government-provided social safety net programs would outweigh the increase in government tax revenue	✘ Immigration has had little positive or negative effect on GDP ✔ Immigrants tend to be more of an asset than a burden to budgets ✔ The younger the immigrant population and the better access they have to the labor market, the more productive they are

The Heritage Foundation's economic analysis of immigration reform drew a markedly different conclusion than AAF, CAP, or the Cato Institute. The Heritage Foundation's study found that immigration reform could result in increased use of direct benefits, means-tested welfare benefits, public education, and population-based services, such as police and fire department services.[185] The foundation's report argues that this increased use of services would place a greater fiscal burden on current U.S. citizens, as "lawful immigrant households receive significantly more welfare, on average, than U.S.-born households."[186] By taking into account the increased access to government services newly-legalized immigrants would receive, the study finds that "former unlawful immigrants together would receive $9.4 trillion in government benefits and services and pay $3.1 trillion in taxes," increasing the

183 Daniel Griswold, "The Fiscal Impact of Immigration Reform: the Real Story," Cato Institute, May 21, 2007, http://www.cato.org/publications/free-trade-bulletin/fiscal-impact-immigration-reform-real-story.
184 Ibid.
185 Robert Rector and Jacob Richwine, "The Fiscal Cost of Unlawful Immigrants and Amnesty to the U.S. Taxpayer," the Heritage Foundation, May 6, 2013, http://www.heritage.org/research/reports/2013/05/the-fiscal-cost-of-unlawful-immigrants-and-amnesty-to-the-us-taxpayer.
186 Ibid.

deficit by $6.3 trillion.[187] As a result, the Heritage Foundation deemed immigration reform to be to the economic disadvantage, rather than benefit, of the United States.

The Center for Immigration Studies' report on the fiscal impact of immigration begins with stating the Heritage Foundation's report is "the most detailed and exhaustive ever done on this topic."[188] It goes on to echo much of the Heritage Foundation's analysis, finding that the financial burden of increased use of governmental services and welfare programs that would result from granting illegal immigrants legal status would outweigh the increased tax revenue brought in by the same action.

CIS's report goes on to defend the Heritage Foundation's study, responding to criticism that the foundation's study used non-standard methodology. Critics of the Heritage Foundation's conclusions have argued that the study overestimated the welfare usage of immigrant families by examining taxes paid and services used on a household rather than individual basis. Doing so included U.S.-born children, who would not theoretically increase the welfare burden, already being legal citizens. Unlike the Heritage Foundation, the Cato Institute calculates the difference between services used and taxes paid on an individual basis, a factor that contributes to the two organization's decidedly different conclusions on the economic impacts of immigration reform. CIS also disputes the Cato Institute's claim that the increased population growth caused by immigration would result in increased GDP growth, compounding the differences between the two reports.

In between these organizations stands the OECD, whose findings state that immigration has little effect on the economy.[189] In developed countries, "the current impact of the cumulative waves of migration that arrived over the past 50 years is just not that large, whether on the positive or negative side."[190] In its survey of member countries, the OECD found that immigrants were more of a financial asset than liability, though in terms of public expenditure relative to GDP, their effect was minimal, not exceeding 0.5 percent of GDP in either direction.[191] The OECD study did find, however, that younger immigrant populations, such as those found in the United States, generally had a positive fiscal impact and that the amount of economic benefit to society provided by immigrants was directly proportional to accessibility of the labor market.

Ultimately, however, the budgetary effects of immigration reform, whatever form it may take, are best summed up by CBO in its report: "[T]he effects of S. 744 on the economy and the federal budget would be complicated and highly uncertain, even in the short run, and as a result the actual effects could be well outside CBO's ranges."[192] In the case of immigration policy, at least, economic calculating and conjecturing can only go so far.

★

187 Ibid.
188 Steven A. Camarota, "The Fiscal Impact of Immigration," the Center for Immigration Studies, May 2013, http://www.cis.org/OpedsandArticles/Camarota-Heritage-Immigration.
189 David Jolly, "Immigration Cost to Countries Is Overstated, Study Finds," *New York Times*, June 13, 2013, http://www.nytimes.com/2013/06/14/business/global/immigration-costs-are-overstated-study-finds.html.
190 Ibid.
191 Ibid.
192 Page 14, "The Economic Impact of S. 744, the Border Security, Economic Opportunity, and Immigration Modernization Act," Congressional Budget Office, June 2013, http://www.cbo.gov/sites/default/files/cbofiles/attachments/44346-Immigration.pdf.

by Priyanka Menon

SEQUESTRATION'S EFFECT ON EDUCATION

Like most other federal department and agencies, the Department of Education (ED) did not escape unscathed from the March 1, 2013 budget cuts. Overall, sequestration meant a reduction of 5.1 percent in ED funding, equal to $2.6 billion in spending cuts, in FY 2013.[193] However, because most ED programs are structured around the school year rather than fiscal year calendars, the impact of the 2013 sequestration budget cuts is being felt in the 2013-2014, rather than 2012-2013, school year.

Pell Grants were the only ED program to be completely exempted from the budget cuts, while programs such as Head Start and Impact Aid lost $406 million and $58.8 million in funding, respectively.[194] These funding cuts have translated into reduced capacity and services for the affected programs. In response to the sequestration mandated cuts, Head Start centers across the nation collectively reduced pay for or laid off 18,000 employees, removed 1.3 million days of programming from their calendars, and stopped providing services to 57,000 children in preparation for the 2013 school year.[195]

Impact Aid is the ED program that provides federal money to school districts whose boundaries include or are near large portions of federal lands such as Indian territories or military bases.[196] Because these areas are not required to pay local property taxes, Impact Aid aims to close the funding caused by this exemption.[197] The 2013 sequestration cut around $60 million from Impact Aid's budget, meaning schools dependent on the federal money must cut programs, lay off teachers, and reduce supplies. Jack Boogaard, assistant superintendent of Central Union Schools District in California, told NPR that the sequestration cuts to Impact Aid also made planning for the future difficult, resulting in last minute staffing and curriculum changes.[198] Because Impact Aid is one of the few ED programs that is not forward funded, the effects of the sequestration cuts were felt immediately, so districts and administrators had to cope with budget reductions mid-year.[199]

FY 2014

Moving into FY 2014, President Obama's budget proposal sidestepped the possibility of continued budget cuts, instead looking to build on the initiatives of his first term. The funding request for ED totaled $71.2 billion for FY 2014, a 3.1 percent increase over 2012 levels.[200]

193 "Help Stop Sequestration," National Association of Elementary School Principals, http://www.naesp.org/sequestration-resource-page#loc2.
194 Ibid.
195 Michael Alison Chandler, "Head Start eliminated services to 57,000 children in U.S. as a result of sequester," *Washington Post*, August 18, 2013, http://www.washingtonpost.com/local/education/head-start-eliminated-services-to-57000-children-in-us-as-a-result-of-sequester/2013/08/18/e1181810-06d9-11e3-9259-e2aafe5a5f84_story.html.
196 "About Impact Aid," U.S. Department of Education, http://www2.ed.gov/about/offices/list/oese/impactaid/whatisia.html.
197 Ibid.
198 Kelly McEvers, "Schools On Military Bases Also Fall Victim To Sequester Cuts," National Public Radio, May 4, 2013 http://www.npr.org/2013/05/04/181168667/schools-on-military-bases-also-fall-victim-to-sequester-cuts.
199 Arne Duncan, "Possible Impact of Sequestration," testimony before the committee on Appropriations, U.S. Senate, February 14, 2013 https://www.ed.gov/news/speeches/testimony-secretary-arne-duncan-senate-appropriations-committee-possible-impact-seques.
200 Arne Duncan, Department of Education statement, testimony before the Senate Budget Committee, U.S. Senate, June 18, 2013.

DEPARTMENT OF EDUCATION BUDGET OUTLAYS, 1981 - 2023

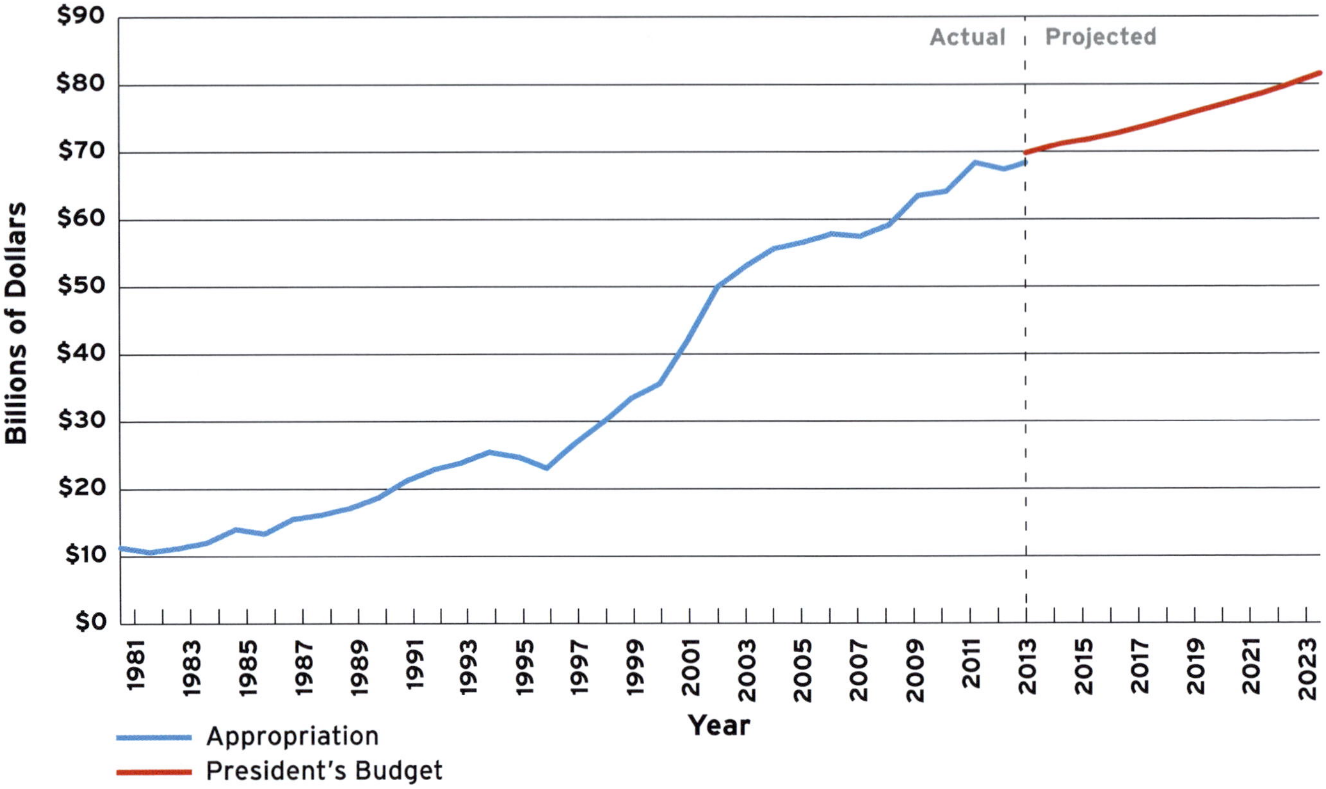

FIGURE 32 SOURCE: U.S. Department of Education and Office of Management and Budget, http://www.gpo.gov/fdsys/pkg/BUDGET-2014-BUD/pdf/BUDGET-2014-BUD.pdf and http://www2.ed.gov/about/overview/budget/history/edhistory.pdf.

Among the administration's main focuses are early childhood education, STEM education, and higher education. In each of these areas, President Obama set forth proposals that promise to significantly modify ED's programs in these fields.

"Preschool for All"

Perhaps the most dramatic aspect of Obama's education budget is his request of $75 billion in mandatory spending for early childhood education over the next ten years, with $1.3 billion requested for 2014.[201] This mandatory investment, which would fund the president's "Preschool for All" initiative, is accompanied by a $750 million request in discretionary funding for Preschool Development Grants.[202] Together, these programs represent the largest increase in federal funding to early childhood education since 1965, the year of Head Start's creation.[203]

The Preschool for All initiative would create a federal-state partnership that incentivizes states to provide a preschool education to all 4-year olds residing within their borders. Federal funds would be awarded to states in proportion to their share of 4-year olds from families at or below 200 percent the federal poverty line,[204] with the money subsequently given to school districts and other partners to create universally accessible preschool programs.[205] In

201 The President's 2014 Budget Proposal for Education, U.S. Department of Education.
202 "Fiscal Year 2014 Budget Summary and Background Information," U.S. Department of Education, http://www2.ed.gov/about/overview/budget/budget14/summary/14summary.pdf.
203 Transcript of "A Conversation with Arne Duncan at the Brookings Institute".
204 "Fiscal Year 2014 Budget Summary."
205 "Investing in Early Learning," U.S. Department of Education, http://www2.ed.gov/about/overview/budget/budget14/crosscuttingissues/earlylearning.pdf.

turn, the programs created by the state and its partnering school districts must meet eight requirements set out by the federal government, among which are small class sizes and a high teacher-to-student ratio, a full day program, staff salaries at levels comparable to those of K-12 staff, and frequent program evaluations.[206] Though the federal government would initially bear the brunt of the costs of these programs, states would be expected to assume these costs over time.[207]

The Obama administration has cited a "focus on [return on investment]" as "key justification for President Obama's groundbreaking preschool proposal."[208] The Department of Education's FY 2014 Budget Summary and Background Information stated that, for "every $1 invested in high-quality preschool, taxpayers saved an average of more than $7 in future costs due to reduction in remedial education costs, increased labor productivity, and reduced crime."[209] Children enrolled in high-quality early childhood education programs are more likely to graduate from school and hold a job than their unenrolled counterparts.[210] [211]

PUBLIC SPENDING ON PRE-PRIMARY EDUCATION BY COUNTRY

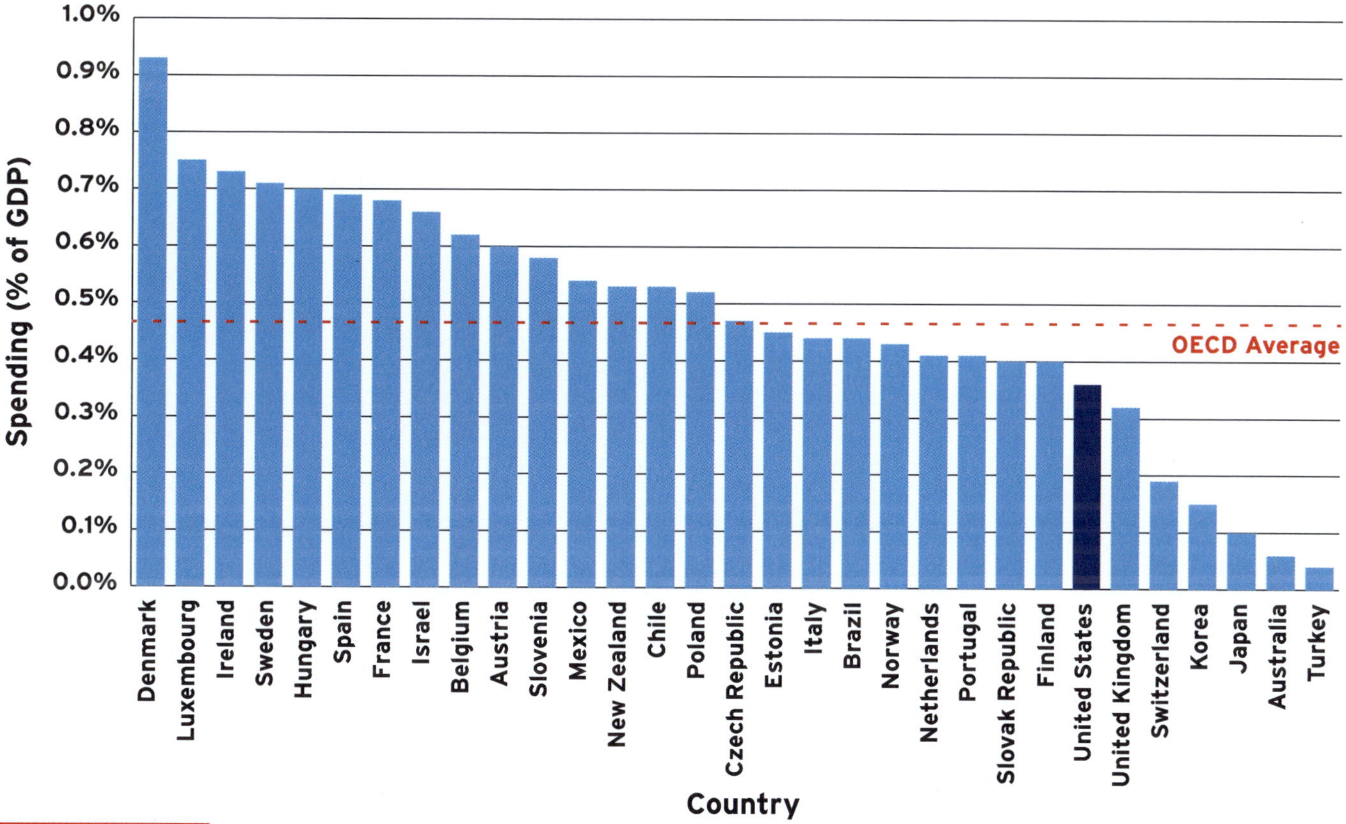

FIGURE 33 SOURCE: Organisation for Economic Co-operation and Development, http://www.oecd.org/edu/eag2013%20(eng)--FINAL%2020%20June%202013.pdf.

206 "Fiscal Year 2014 Budget Summary and Background Information," U.S. Department of Education, http://www2.ed.gov/about/overview/budget/budget14/summary/14summary.pdf.
207 Ibid.
208 Arne Duncan, Department of Education statement, testimony before the Senate Budget Committee, U.S. Senate, June 18, 2013.
209 "Fiscal Year 2014 Budget Summary and Background Information."
210 Ibid.
211 Arne Duncan, Department of Education statement, testimony before the Senate Budget Committee, U.S. Senate, June 18, 2013.

Not everyone is as optimistic about these projections, however. Grover Whitehurst, Director of the Brown Center on Education Policy at the Brookings Institute, told ARUSA that a seven-to-one ROI was "unrealistic."[212] He pointed out that the administration's oft cited seven-to-one figure is primarily based on the findings of the HighScope Perry Preschool Study, known as the Perry Preschool Project, a program that took place in Yspilanti, Michigan in 1960s and examined the lives of 123 children born into families below the poverty line and who were at high risk of failing high school.[213] The study randomly assigned a subset of the children to receive high quality preschool education from ages 3 to 4, subsequently documenting the differences between those children who received an early childhood education and those who received none. The study found that the preschool program had a significant positive impact on the children over the short and long terms, finding "a return to society of more than $16 for every tax dollar invested in the early care and education program."[214]

Whitehurst, however, maintained that there are large differences between Obama's proposed program and the Perry Preschool Project. "Perry was an expensive two-year intervention that required participant mothers not to work outside the home and included parent counseling," Whitehurst stated. "It served only African-American children from very low-income families at a time when there were virtually no other preschool services available, not even Sesame Street," he added.[215] On the other hand, the programs funded by Preschool for All aim to serve children from a multitude of socio-economic and racial backgrounds and lack several components, not to mention the funding, of the Perry Preschool Project. Consequently, the figures generated by the Obama administration, which equate Preschool for All to the Perry Preschool Project, overestimate the impact of Preschool for All, meaning that the ROI of Preschool for All is "likely to be much lower than seven-to-one."[216]

STEM Education

The president's budget also makes substantial changes to the structure of STEM (science, technology, engineering, and mathematics) education, fundamentally restructuring over a hundred programs run by 13 agencies.[217] The initiative aims to consolidate these 90 programs into ones overseen by the Department of Education, the National Science Foundation, and the Smithsonian Institution.[218] Through this reconsolidation, ED estimates that around $180 million will be redirected towards the STEM education programs from these three agencies.[219] These redirected funds, on top of additional discretionary funding requested in FY 2014 budget, total an additional investment of $285 million in STEM education on ED's behalf (Figure 34).[220]

Despite the administration's assurances that the quality and scope of current STEM education programs would be maintained by the restructuring, several skeptics remain. After reviewing the president's proposal, the Senate Appropriations Committee released a report that stated it "is not convinced that the quality of these programs would be maintained if they were moved to other Federal agencies."[221] Though the committee supports the administration's focus on efficiency and consolidation, it is concerned that "the proposal as a whole has not been

212 Grover Whitehurst, email message to the author, August 15th, 2013.
213 "Lifetime Effects: The HighScope Perry Preschool Study Through Age 40 (2005)," HighScope, http://www.highscope.org/content.asp?ContentId=219.
214 "HighScope Perry Preschool Study," HighScope, http://www.highscope.org/Content.asp?ContentId=282.
215 Grover Whitehurst, email message to the author, August 15th, 2013.
216 Ibid.
217 "Fiscal Year 2014 Budget Summary and Background Information," U.S. Department of Education, http://www2.ed.gov/about/overview/budget/budget14/summary/14summary.pdf.
218 Page 6, Department of Education funding highlights.
219 Ibid.
220 "Fiscal Year 2014 Budget Summary and Background Information."
221 Bonnie Richman, "Obama Budget Threatens Popular STEM Education Initiatives," *Scientific American*, July 24, 2013 http://www.scientificamerican.com/article.cfm?id=obama-budget-threatens-popular-stem-education-initiatives.

thoroughly vetted with the education community or congressional authorizing committees."[222] Consequently, the committee views the current proposal as eliminating numerous successful and meaningful STEM education programs with "no evaluation on why they were deemed duplicative or ineffective."[223]

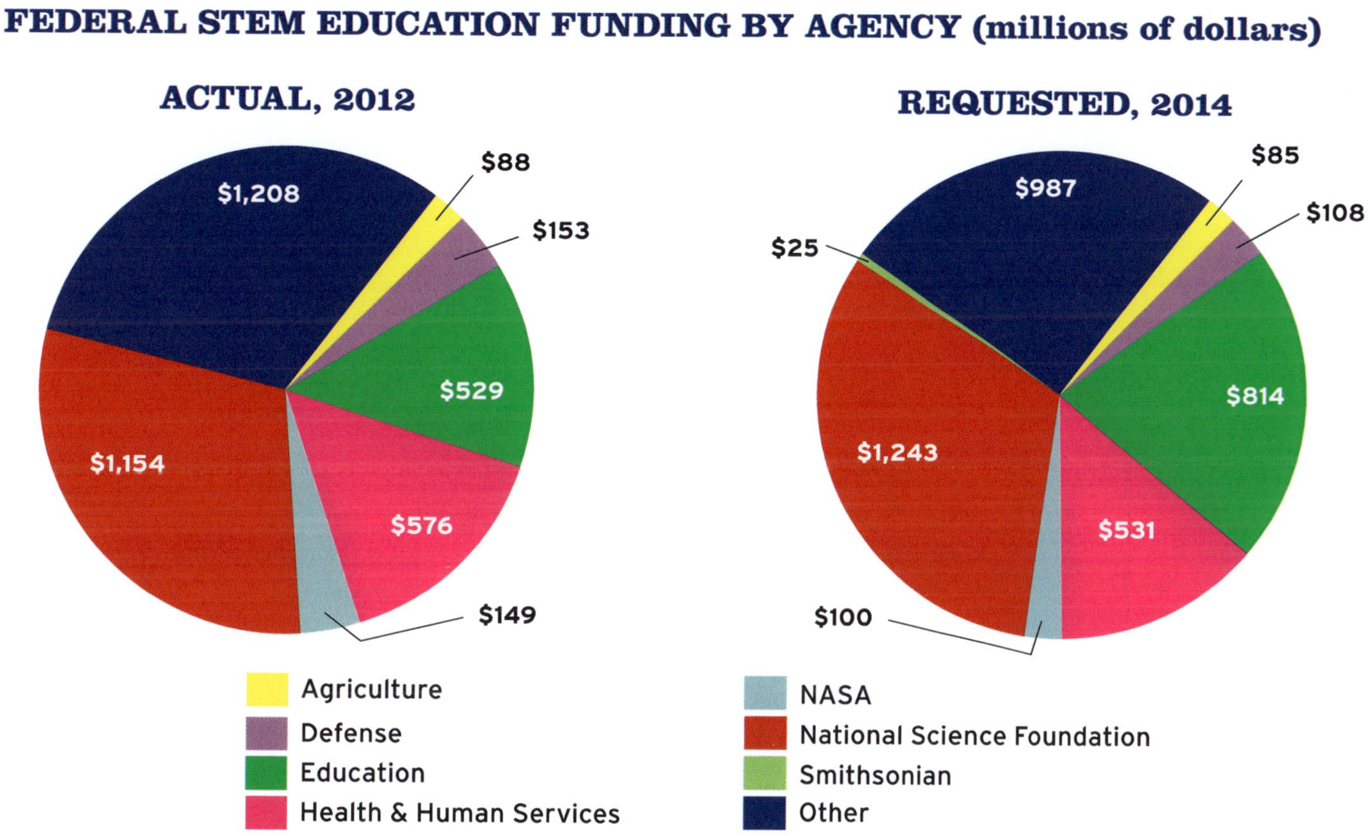

FIGURE 34 SOURCE: National Science and Technology Council, http://www.whitehouse.gov/sites/default/files/microsites/ostp/stem_stratplan_2013.pdf.

Congress isn't the only one critical of Obama's proposed restructuring. Educators around the nation are responding with surprise at the administration's decision to cut programs they find highly beneficial to STEM education in their classrooms. Jeanne Ting Chowning of the Northwest Association for Biomedical Research, an organization that provides kids with STEM related opportunities both in the classroom and out of it, and whose receives more than half of its budget from the federal government, recently told the *Scientific American* that the administration's proposal has sparked panic as her organizations and numerous other ones similar to it race to find homes for the curricula developed by the NIH's Office of Science Education before it shuts its doors as a result of the planned restructuring.[224] "It really is an emergency," Chowning told the magazine.

222 Richard M. Jones, "FYI: The AIP Bulletin of Science Policy News," American Institute of Physics, July 25, 2013, http://www.aip.org/fyi/2013/126.html.
223 Ibid.
224 Bonnie Richman, "Obama Budget Threatens Popular STEM Education Initiatives," *Scientific American*, July 24, 2013 http://www.scientificamerican.com/article.cfm?id=obama-budget-threatens-popular-stem-education-initiatives.

Higher Education

Obama's recently unveiled higher education proposal pushes the federal government to a level of involvement with higher education heretofore unseen, causing it to gain a lot of attention. *Washington Post's* WonkBlog, for one, called the proposal "a really big deal."[225]

Much of the proposal functions around the administration's new college rankings system, which rankings colleges based on accessibility, affordability, and outcomes.[226] In order to quantitatively capture these three qualities, the administration includes figures such as the number of students receiving Pell grants, average tuition, loan debt, graduation rates, graduate degrees, and advanced degrees of college graduates within its scorecard.[227]

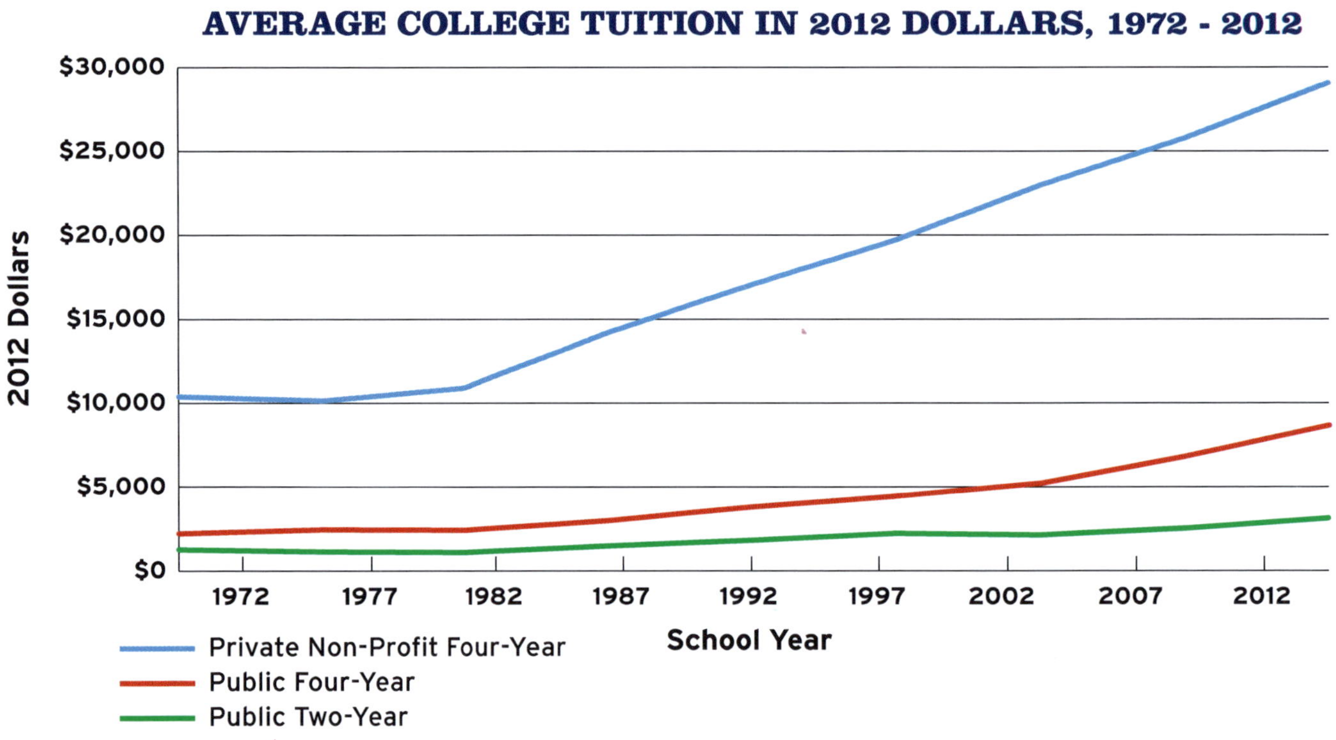

FIGURE 35 SOURCE: The College Board, http://trends.collegeboard.org/college-pricing/figures-tables/tuition-and-fee-and-room-and-board-charges-over-time-1972-73-through-2012-13-selected-years.

The data used in the rankings are not groundbreaking; a majority of components of the scorecard are publically available. However, the administration's move to use this data to rank colleges definitely is. Obama's proposal to institute a system of rating colleges based on accessibility and affordability is new ground for the federal government, stepping into territory that has thus far been dominated by the *U.S. News and World Report*.

In addition, the administration's plan to base the amount of federal aid students receive upon their university's rankings means that once implemented, the system will have a sizable financial impact on universities. Such a move would incentivize students to attend better-ranked universities and incentivize low-performing schools to improve

225 Dylan Matthews, "Everything you need to know about Obama's higher ed plan," *Washington Post*, August 22, 2103, http://www.washingtonpost.com/blogs/wonkblog/wp/2013/08/22/everything-you-need-to-know-about-obamas-higher-ed-plan/.

226 "FACT SHEET on the President's Plan to Make College More Affordable: A Better Bargain for the Middle Class," The White House, August 22, 2013, http://www.whitehouse.gov/the-press-office/2013/08/22/fact-sheet-president-s-plan-make-college-more-affordable-better-bargain-.

227 Ibid.

along the administration's ranking metrics. Though the president has yet to announce how specifically the ratings will impact the federal financial aid given to students, the White House has stated that, "the Administration will seek legislation using this new rating system to transform the way federal aid is awarded to colleges once the ratings are well developed."[228] Much of this effort is focused on redirecting federal aid received by for-profit colleges, who have lower graduation rates and higher tuition than not-for-profit colleges and universities.[229]

★

228 Ibid.
229 Dylan Matthews, "Harkin: For-profit colleges a terrible deal," *Washington Post*, July 30, 2012, http://www.washingtonpost.com/blogs/wonkblog/wp/2012/07/30/harkin-for-profit-colleges-a-terrible-deal/.

EDUCATION, SCIENCE AND TECHNOLOGY: SCIENCE

by Jacob Drucker

The federal government is the largest source of funding for scientific endeavors of all stripes. Through a variety of facets, the government funds research toward everything from robotics to disease prevention. Nevertheless, it is nearly impossible to assign an exact number for the amount of federal money spent on science in FY 2013. Scientific endeavors are scattered across a variety of government agencies, ranging from research and development at the Department of Defense to the aptly named Office of Science, which falls under the broader umbrella of the Department of Energy. Furthermore, until recently, the government had not enacted a formal budget in years, being funded instead by a series of continuing resolutions.

Attempts to quantify federal expenditures on the sciences are further complicated by the budget sequestration, which went into effect on March 1, 2013 and cut $85 billion from the FY 2013 budget. Funding for science and related fields was particularly hard hit by the budget cuts, which sent agencies from NASA to the Center for Disease Control reeling.

SPACE AND ATMOSPHERIC PROGRAM

When taxpayers think of federally funded science programs, their imaginations typically turn to the stars. Since the height of the Cold War, the National Aeronautics and Space Administration (NASA) has cemented itself as the paradigm of successful government forays into scientific research and application: the United States put a man on the moon decades before man thought to put wheels on the suitcase. However, NASA has seen its budget cut significantly for the past several years. In 2011, the Kennedy Space Center ended the space shuttle program amidst tightening budgets, resulting in 8,000 jobs lost on Florida's Space Coast.[230] And the sequestration, which began in March, threatened to delay existing programs well into the future.[231] For FY 2012, NASA's budget was approved by Congress at $17.8 billion.[232] If sequestration remains in effect, its annual outlays for the foreseeable future will total $16.9 billion, roughly 8 percent less than NASA's FY 2011 budget of $18.4 billion. To make up the difference, NASA will cut back across the board, and plans to issue 5 percent fewer research grants.

Of course, as is the case with many federal programs, space exploration depends on other factors and appropriations as well. Take, for instance, the batteries used in explorers such as the Voyager 1 spacecraft. Filled with plutonium-238, they have powered the craft for decades, succeeding where chemical or solar systems failed. The entire American scientific community only has around 36 pounds of plutonium-328 left, a byproduct of Cold War-era weapons-grade plutonium-239 production.[233] Production has recently begun again, but at a rate of only a few pounds a year.[234] NASA's Mars rover Curiosity alone contains 10 pounds of the substance. Russia is rumored to be out of plutonium-238 as well, meaning that NASA simply cannot continue deep-space exploration unless Congress appropriates funds to the Department of Energy for the production of the plutonium isotope.

---

230 Donna Leinwand Leger, "End of shuttle program slams Space Coast economy," *USA Today*, July 5, 2011, http://usatoday30.usatoday.com/money/economy/2011-07-01-space-coast-business_n.htm.

231 Ledyard King, "NASA: Sequestration threatens timetable for projects," *USA Today*, April 23, 2013, http://www.usatoday.com/story/news/politics/2013/04/23/sequestration-threatens-nasa-deadlines/2107585/.

232 Dan Leone, "NASA would take a hit with sequestration," NBC News, Feb. 27, 2013, http://science.nbcnews.com/_news/2013/02/27/17122242-nasa-would-take-a-hit-with-sequestration.

233 Dave Mosher, "NASA's Plutonium Problem Could End Deep-Space Exploration," *Wired*, Sept. 19, 2013, http://www.wired.com/wiredscience/2013/09/plutonium-238-problem/.

234 Shaunacy Ferro, "NASA Resumes Production Of Plutonium-238 Space Fuel After 25 Years," *Popular Science*, March 14, 2013, http://www.popsci.com/science/article/2013-03/first-time-cold-war-us-making-plutonium-238.

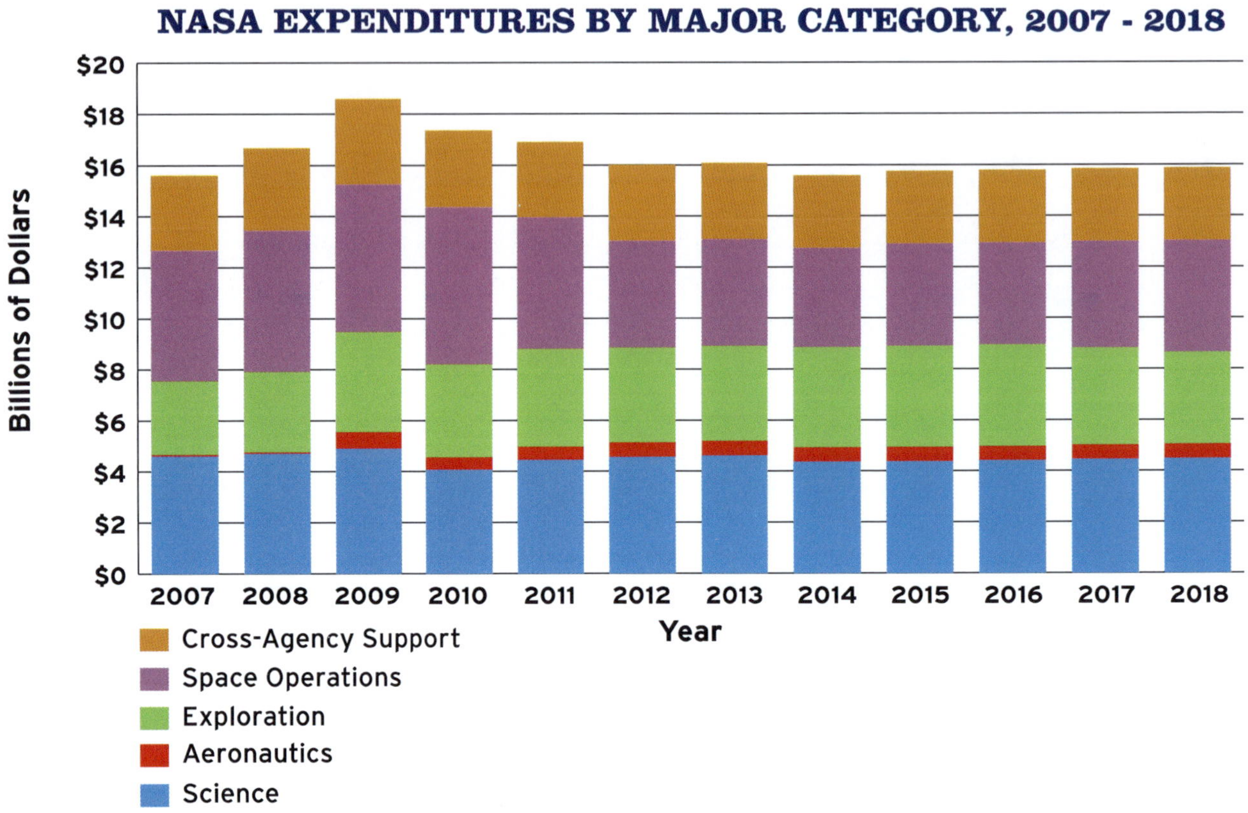

FIGURE 36

SOURCE: National Aeuronautics and Space Administration, http://www.nasa.gov/pdf/210019main_NASA_FY09_Budget_Estimates.pdf, http://www.nasa.gov/pdf/420990main_FY_201_%20Budget_Overview_1_Feb_2010.pdf, http://www.nasa.gov/pdf/516674main_FY12Budget_Estimates_Overview.pdf, http://www.nasa.gov/pdf/632697main_NASA_FY13_Budget_Summary-508.pdf, http://www.nasa.gov/pdf/740512main_FY2014%20CJ%20for%20Online.pdf.

NASA is hardly the only scientific agency to suffer budget cuts from sequestration. The National Oceanic and Atmospheric Administration (NOAA), in many ways NASA's sister organization, was forced to cut over 7 percent of its budget. NOAA's FY 2012 budget was roughly $4.9 billion, about the same as its FY 2013 budget.[235] [236] NOAA has requested a FY 2014 budget of $5.4 billion, an amount that it almost certainly will not receive. In fact, NOAA was scheduled to furlough 12,000 of its workers for four days in July and August, a plan that was ultimately canceled due to a spate of deadly tornadoes and NOAA's need to remain fully operational during the stormy summer months.[237] To make up the loss, the agency proposed taking money from its weather satellite program.[238]

DEPARTMENT OF HEALTH AND HUMAN SERVICES

The list of scientific endeavors affected continues. The Department of Health and Human Services (HHS) faced the second largest sequestration-created budget cut at $6.57 billion, behind only the Department of Defense.[239] Of that total, $490 million was sequestered from the Centers for Disease Control and Prevention (CDC), one of

235 "OMB Report Pursuant to the Sequestration Transparency Act of 2012," http://www.whitehouse.gov/sites/default/files/omb/assets/legislative_reports/stareport.pdf.
236 "2014 Budget Summary," NOAA, http://www.corporateservices.noaa.gov/nbo/fy14_bluebook/FINALnoaaBlueBook_2014_Web_Full.pdf.
237 Dashiell Bennett, "All These Tornadoes Mean No More Sequester Furloughs at NOAA," the *Atlantic Wire*, June 3, 2013, http://www.theatlanticwire.com/national/2013/06/tornadoes-sequester-furloughs-noaa/65811/.
238 David Rogers, "Stalled takeoff for NOAA satellite plan?" Politico, June 9, 2013, http://www.politico.com/story/2013/06/bumpy-landing-for-noaa-satellite-plan-92468.html.
239 "What Gets Cut in Sequestration," Here and Now- WBUR, Dec. 14, 2012, http://hereandnow.wbur.org/2012/12/04/sequestration-spending-cuts.

the dozen agencies that make up HHS. The CDC cut $40 million in HIV prevention and $25 million that went toward global efforts to eliminate polio and prevent outbreaks of measles, malaria, and pandemic flu.[240] Not all agencies within HHS were affected equally, though. The Agency for Healthcare Research and Quality escaped unscathed from the sequestration, and has essentially the same budget as it did in FY 2012: a bit under $400 million.[241] For FY 2014, HHS requested tens of billions of dollars for research expenditures.

REQUESTED RESEARCH EXPENDITURES BY DEPARTMENT, 2014 (millions of dollars)

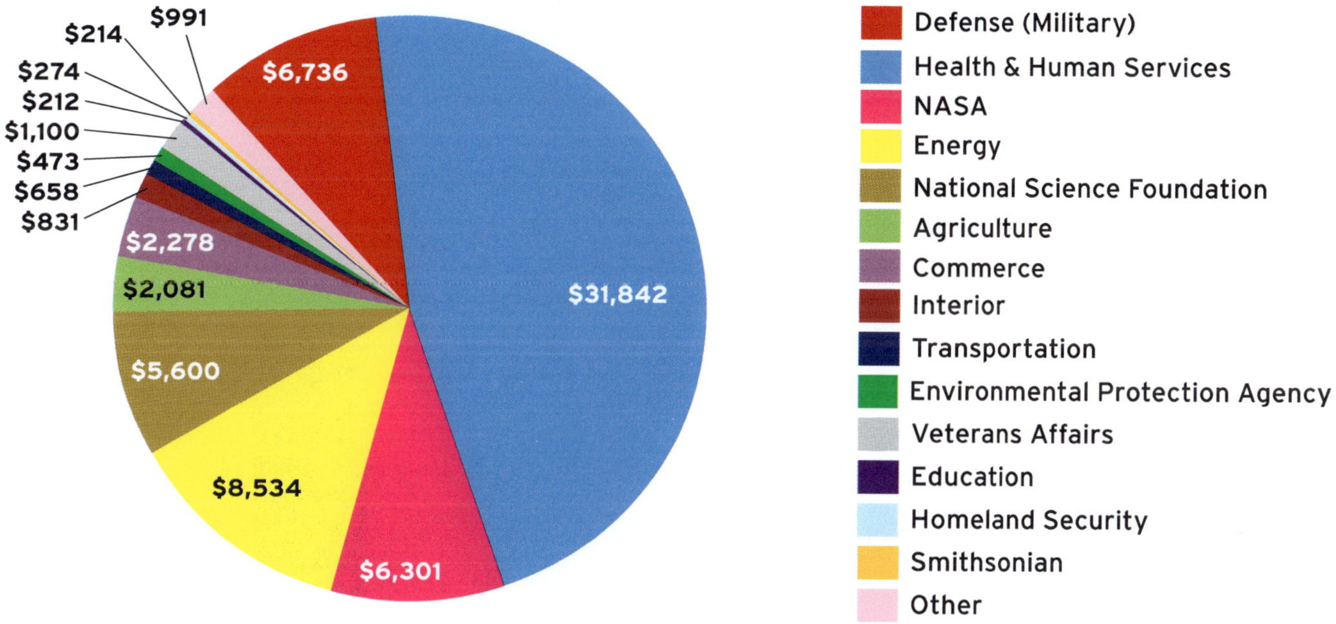

FIGURE 37 SOURCE: White House Office of Science and Technology Policy, http://www.whitehouse.gov/sites/default/files/microsites/ostp/2014_R&Dbudget_overview.pdf.

The Food and Drug Administration (FDA), another part of HHS, had its budget cut by the sequestration as well, forcing the agency to scale back. The cuts meant that the FDA had to restrict the number of staffers it sent to the Food and Drug Law Institute's annual meeting in April. The conference, though, was just a subway ride away from FDA headquarters in Washington, D.C. The FDA reconfigured its budget to avoid cutting back on food inspections, so as to impose no additional risk to public safety. However, the full effects of its smaller budget will not be felt until 2014 and beyond.[242]

A much larger cut hit the National Institutes of Health (NIH), to the tune of over $2.5 billion, leading the institute to fund 700 fewer competitive research grants than it did in 2012.[243] Bear in mind that the NIH funds about a quarter of all biomedical research in the U.S.[244] According to the American Association for the Advancement of

240 "Fact Sheet: Impact of Sequestration and Other Budget Changes on the Centers for Disease Control and Prevention," CDC, http://www.cdc.gov/fmo/topic/Budget%20Information/appropriations_budget_form_pdf/Sequester_Impacts.pdf.
241 "Agency for Healthcare Research and Quality (AHRQ)," Association of American Medical Colleges, https://www.aamc.org/advocacy/budget/176448/agencyforhealthcareresearchandquality.html.
242 "Statement Regarding Potential Budget Cuts to the FDA and NIH," Alliance for Regenerative Medicine, http://alliancerm.org/statement-regarding-potential-budget-cuts-fda-and-nih.
243 "OMB Report Pursuant to the Sequestration Transparency Act of 2012," http://www.whitehouse.gov/sites/default/files/omb/assets/legislative_reports/stareport.pdf.
244 Jonathan Cohn, "The Sequester is Stifling Science," New Republic, August 15, 2013, http://www.newrepublic.com/article/114316/sequestration-impact-nih-nsf-and-scientific-research.

Science, the sequestration decreased spending on research and development throughout the nation by a whopping $9.3 billion in just this past fiscal year alone, and the effects will continue in future years.[245]

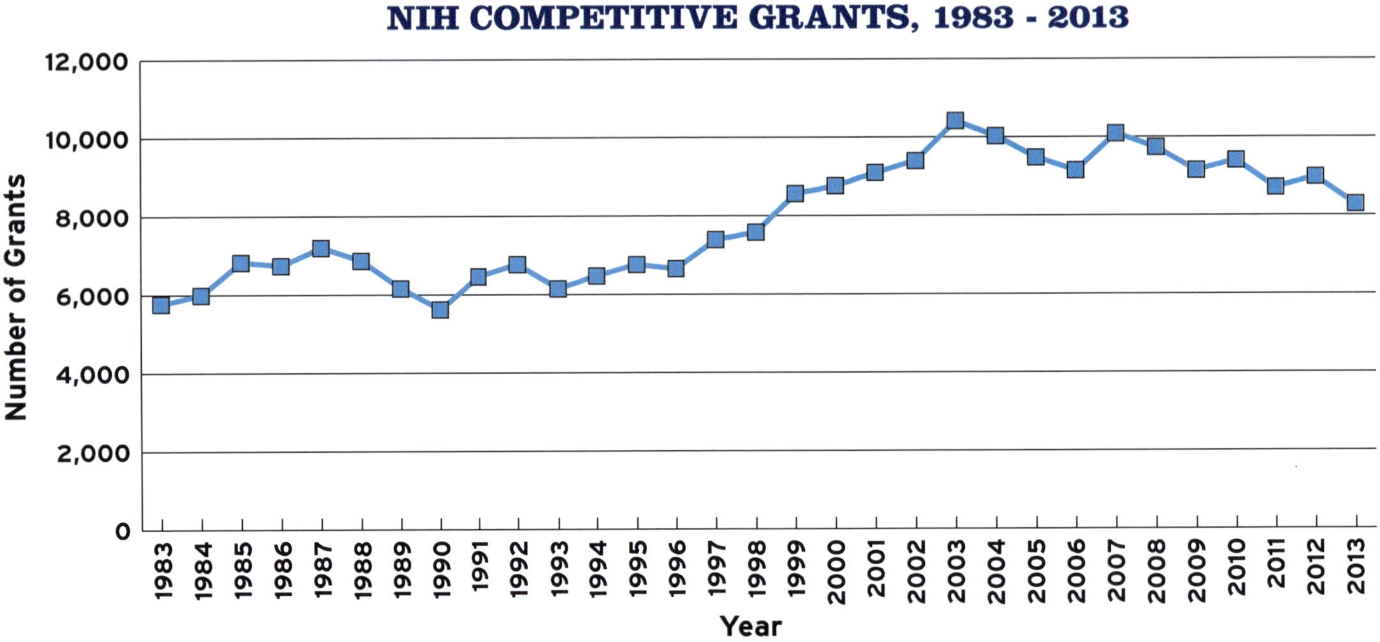

FIGURE 38

SOURCE: National Institutes of Health, http://officeofbudget.od.nih.gov/pdfs/spending_history/Mechanism%20Detail%20for%20Total%20NIH%20FY%201983%20-%20FY%201999.pdf, http://officeofbudget.od.nih.gov/pdfs/spending_history/Mechanism%20Detail%20for%20Total%20NIH%20FY%202000%20-%20FY%202012%20(3).pdf and http://officeofbudget.od.nih.gov/pdfs/FY13/FY%202013%20Full-Year%20NIH%20Mechanism%20Table%20Posting%20.pdf.

Sheila Jasanoff, professor of science and technology at Harvard University, expressed grave concern regarding the federal budget cuts to the NIH. "Everybody's incredibly fearful about where things are going. There's no question that the scientific community is very fearful."[246] Jasanoff emphasized the scope of the budget cuts, which threaten even neuroscience. "Even that area, which enjoys high [bipartisan] support, is being cut. Brain research has widespread support, high levels of political support, there's a great deal of interest, and even MIT scientists on brain research are running scared."

Thousands of scientists recently responded to a survey conducted by the American Society for Biochemistry and Molecular Biology regarding sequestration's effects on their work, and more than three quarters of them have reported that they spend more time writing grant proposals than they did in 2010.[247] Over 60 percent of respondents, however, reported a decrease in funding level in the equivalent time period. Funding has become more competitive, and two-thirds of respondents agreed with the statement, "I do not have the funds to expand our research operations." Of these respondents, over 90 percent work in academia, and only 3 percent work as

245 Sam Stein, "Sequester Impact on Medical Research Results In Cuts To Promising Projects," *Huffington Post*, May 2, 2013, http://www.huffingtonpost.com/2013/05/02/sequester-impact-medical-research_n_3203089.html.
246 Sheila Jasanoff, interview by author, Sept. 30, 2013.
247 "Unlimited Potential, Vanishing Opportunity," Survey conducted by the American Society for Biochemistry and Molecular Biology, summer of 2013, http://www.asbmb.org/uploadedFiles/Advocacy/Events/UPVO%20Survey%20Data.pdf.

government researchers. At the University of Chicago, for instance, three laboratories were closed due to NIH funding cuts.[248]

DEPARTMENT OF ENERGY

With all said and done, the Office of Science, an agency within the Department of Energy, endured a $215 million decrease in funding from FY 2012 to FY 2013 on a budget of around $5 billion.[249] In his statement to Congress in March, Office of Science Chairman William Brinkman detailed sequestration-induced cuts. "In the Biological and Environmental Research Program…three funding opportunity announcements will be cancelled, impacting potentially over 25 grants. In High Energy Physics, Fermi National Accelerator Laboratory (Fermilab) will face reduced accelerator runtime and staff reductions. Core research will also be reduced." The list went on. The Office of Science's 17 national labs, which trace their roots back to the Manhattan Project, are threatened by the cutbacks.[250]

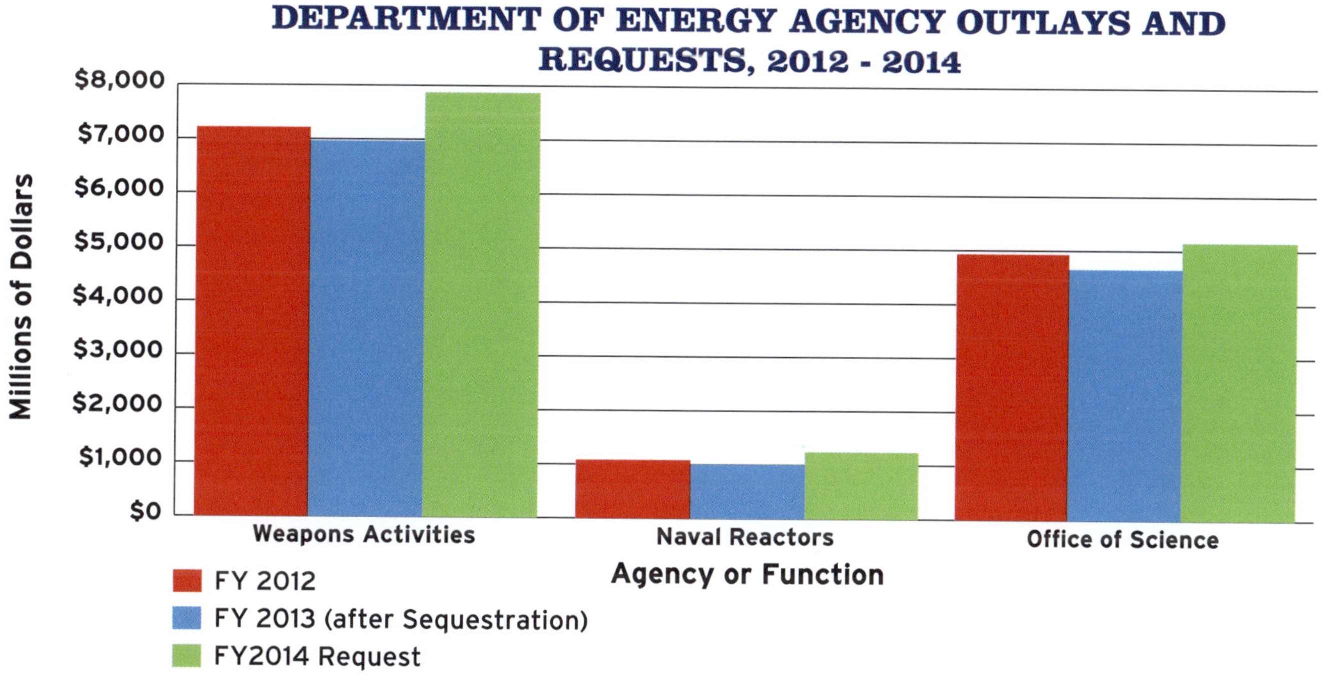

FIGURE 39

SOURCE:Department of Energy and Office of Management and Budget, http://energy.gov/sites/prod/files/2013/04/f0/FY14_DOE_Budget_Highlights_Final.pdf and http://www.whitehouse.gov/sites/default/files/omb/assets/legislative_reports/fy13ombjcsequestrationreport.pdf.

The National Nuclear Security Administration (NNSA) had its budget slashed by over $1 billion by sequestration, the most of any agency in the DoE.[251] President Obama had requested an increase of over $500 million in funding for NNSA in his 2013 budget proposal, but the agency instead found itself with an across the board 9.4 percent budget cut, affecting everything from weapons activities, which faced a loss of $678 million, to naval reactors, which saw its budget slashed by $102 million. The deep cuts to America's nuclear programs could compromise

248 Jennifer Liberto, "Scientists laid off due to budget cuts," CNN Money, Sept. 3, 2013, http://money.cnn.com/2013/09/03/news/science-budget-cuts/index.html.

249 William F. Brinkman, "Statement of Director of the Office of Science," testimony before the Subcommittee on Energy & Water Appropriations, U.S. House of Representatives, March 5, 2013, http://science.energy.gov/~/media/sc-1/pdf/2013/030513_brinkman_sewa.pdf.

250 Darius Dixon, "Sequester looms over storied energy labs," Politico, April 2, 2013, http://www.politico.com/story/2013/04/sequestration-looms-over-storied-energy-labs-89567.html.

251 "OMB Report Pursuant to the Sequestration Transparency Act of 2012," http://www.whitehouse.gov/sites/default/files/omb/assets/legislative_reports/stareport.pdf.

national security. In September 2012, for instance, Halliburton reported having lost a radioactive fuel rod in Texas.[252] Figure 39 displays overall DoE spending levels on similar programs.

Rather than lament the budget cuts, though, some have pointed to wasteful programs that could be cut and expenditures that perhaps should not have been billed to the taxpayer. For example, Senator Tom Coburn (R-Okla.) compiles an annual list of allegedly wasteful spending, including a DoE-funded contest to create a home energy-monitoring app despite the fact that such an app already existed.[253] The DoE also spent federal taxpayer funds retrofitting a VIP yacht in Los Angeles. Those expenditures, though, total less than $600,000, a drop in the nearly $2.5 billion bucket of DoE cuts.[254]

Other Scientific Expenditures

And so, while entitlement programs continue to expand, budget cuts have disproportionately hit federal programs dealing with science and energy. The White House estimates that overall science budgets were cut by over 8 percent by sequestration, a fallback plan designed to be unpalatable enough to force budget negotiations.[255] Consequently, science spending, historically a bipartisan issue, has found itself suffering the consequences of intentionally destructive fiscal policy.

The U.S. Geological Survey (USGS), a bureau of the Department of the Interior, faces an $88M cut to a budget of close to $1.5 billion.[256] To help compensate for the reduced finances, the USGS is in the process of discontinuing 375 stream gages, which measure water elevation and serve as warning systems for flooding as well as measures of water availability.[257] Deputy Chief of the USGS Office of Surface Water Robert Mason explained to *USA Today* that the operating cost of all 8,000 gauges is about $150 million annually.[258]

Looking Forward

It is important to note that President Obama's proposed budget for FY 2014 was considerably more generous toward scientific endeavors than current outlays. He increased funding for the National Science Foundation, DoE's Office of Science, and the National Institute of Standards and Technology, among other programs. Such levels of spending were expected, based on Obama's early promise to "restore science to its rightful place." Professor Jasanoff noted the widespread excitement within the scientific community. After the end of Bush's presidency, she explained, the scientific community expected blue skies in terms of federal funding.[259]

Members of the scientific community praised President Obama's proposed budget.[260] "United for Medical Research (UMR) applauds Obama's proposal to increase funding for the National Institutes of Health," one statement released by the UMR in April 2013 read. The sentiments were mirrored by the American Chemical

252 Kathy Warbelow & Brian Wingfield, "FBI Clears Halliburton Crew in Loss of Radioactive Tool," Bloomberg, September 14, 2012, http://www.bloomberg.com/news/2012-09-13/halliburton-hunting-for-missing-radioactive-probe-in-west-texas.html.
253 Senator Tom Coburn, M.D. "Waste Book," October 2012, http://www.coburn.senate.gov/public/index.cfm?a=Files.Serve&File_id=b7b23f66-2d60-4d5a-8bc5-8522c7e1a40e.
254 "OMB Report Pursuant to the Sequestration Transparency Act of 2012," http://www.whitehouse.gov/sites/default/files/omb/assets/legislative_reports/stareport.pdf.
255 David Malakoff, "Sequestration Would Cut U.S. Science Budgets by 8.2%, White House Estimates," *Science*, September 14, 2012, http://news.sciencemag.org/2012/09/sequestration-would-cut-u.s.-science-budgets-8.2-white-house-estimates.
256 "OMB Report Pursuant to the Sequestration Transparency Act of 2012," http://www.whitehouse.gov/sites/default/files/omb/assets/legislative_reports/stareport.pdf.
257 http://streamstatsags.cr.usgs.gov/ThreatenedGages/ThreatenedGages.html.
258 Doyle Rice, "Up to 375 flood gauges to turn off because of fund cuts," *USA Today*, April 26, 2013, http://www.usatoday.com/story/news/nation/2013/04/25/flood-gauges-sequester/2113141/.
259 Sheila Jasanoff, interview by author, September 30, 2013.
260 "Reactions to Obama's Science Budget," *Sciencemag*, April 12, 2013, http://news.sciencemag.org/2013/04/reactions-obamas-science-budget.

Society (ACS), which responded to the budget proposal with: "The ACS applauds the release of the president's FY14 budget and his continued recognition of the importance of science and technology as the fuel for economic growth and job creation."

The president's budget, though, was simply one proposal, one nearly uniformly acknowledged to have little effect on actual appropriations. His blueprint included significant tax hikes and a deficit of roughly $750 billion that would only decrease to over $400 billion in a decade's time, a political non-starter in today's polarized and deficit-focused Washington.[261] Unfortunately for the scientific community, most of sequestration continues to be the law of the land. Perhaps the 114th Congress will increase appropriations for scientific endeavors. Until then, though, science funding will remain where it is: a somewhat scaled-back version of its more illustrious past.

★

261 "The battle over the 2014 budget," *Washington Post*, April 1, 2013, http://www.washingtonpost.com/wp-srv/special/politics/2014-budget-comparisons/.

AGRICULTURE

by Matt Shuham

The "farm bill"—more formally known as the Agriculture Reform, Food and Jobs Act of 2013 in the Senate, and the Federal Agriculture Reform and Risk Management Act of 2013 in the House of Representatives—refers to the legislation responsible for providing billions of dollars to American farmers in different forms of crop insurance, as well as covering America's national food stamp program, or the Supplemental Nutrition Assistance Program ("SNAP"). The debate surrounding the farm bill covers broad ground, though most contentious is the place SNAP holds in the federal budget.

Historical Context

The farm bill is the primary funding program for the U.S. Department of Agriculture, and it covers most of the agency's operations. Congress renews it approximately every 5 years (the last was passed in 2008), and includes money for payments to farmers, rural development, conservation, nutrition programs, research, and a host of smaller programs. The primary role of the farm bill, since its start in the Great Depression, is to balance out the supply and demand of crops in America. Simply put, the government sometimes pays farmers not to farm, because as supply goes up, price can drop, sometimes levels that would leave many farming families in the below the poverty line. Subsidies to farmers, then, act to ensure that American farmers are never producing more food than they can sell at reasonable prices. In addition to these subsidies, the farm bill includes federally-supported crop insurance: if farmers have an off year, usually because of poor weather conditions, private insurance companies subsidized by the government can help pick up some of the losses. Finally, the farm bill includes payments to farmers struggling for reasons other than those covered by crop insurance. On its face, the farm bill is a pretty good deal for farmers—it lessens the risk of an otherwise financially unstable profession.

Of course, there has always been plenty of debate around the idea of agricultural subsidies: why should the government dictate what farmers should grow, and how much they grow of it? Wouldn't the free market do a better job of regulating the agricultural industry than the inefficient (and sometimes corrupt) leagues of government bureaucrats at the USDA?

Well, yes and no. Critics of the farm bill point to how wasteful it can be: billions of dollars often end up in the hands of large corporate farmers, many of whom make hundreds of thousands of dollars a year. Subsidies also distort supply: subsidies support corn production but pass over many other vegetables, making corn syrup cheap and abundant, and keeping healthier produce out of the reach for poor families. The 2008 farm bill invested lots of money in growing corn for ethanol use, leading some to believe it was responsible, at least in part, for the global food crisis in the same year.

So why, with the majority of polled Americans not in support of farm subsidies, would Congress vote, decade after decade—for 70 years—to keep renewing it? Put simply, there's enormous political power in the agricultural lobby—the interest groups that represent farmer's interests on the national stage. Through millions of dollars in campaign donations and advertising, many of America's wealthiest farming organizations have made it very difficult to change any agricultural policy that benefits their industry. Even though farmers make up only 1 percent of working Americans, they have tremendous political power, and their subsidies have almost always been sacrosanct in Congress. In addition, farmers are very vocal advocates for farm subsidies, while voters that may not support them don't often view it as a very important issue. In other words, it's fairly easy for members of Congress to ignore farm bill detractors, but it's quite difficult to ignore farmers themselves. Finally, it's easy to forget that all farm bills also include enormous amounts of food stamp funding. This garners support from those who might otherwise oppose the farm bill, such as industrial workers or urban interests.

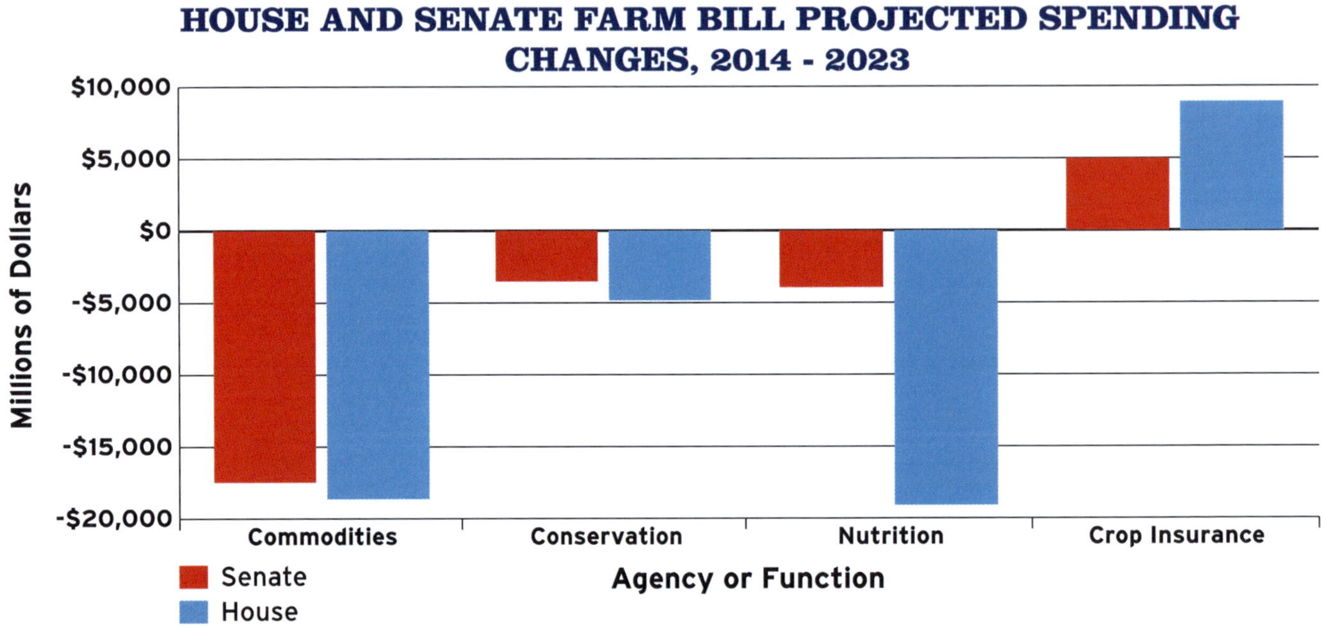

FIGURE 40 SOURCE: Congressional Research Service, http://www.fas.org/sgp/crs/misc/R43076.pdf.

Current Debate

Because of the support for the farm bill, few modifications were proposed this year in the House and Senate. The primary debate in this arena, however, surrounds the food stamp program, SNAP.

The American food stamp program began in 1939, at the tail end of the Great Depression, as a way to use agricultural subsidies to feed the hungry. After ending the program from 1943-1961, it was re-started under President John F. Kennedy's watch as a fulfillment of a campaign promise. By 1965, 500,000 people were using food stamps. In 1973, they were officially included in the farm bill for the first time. Food stamp usage generally follows the economic health of the United States as a whole: lower when times are good, and higher when they are bad.

When the so-called "Great Recession" began in late 2007, food stamp use began to rise. Between then and 2011, average monthly participation grew nearly 77 percent.[262] The cost of the program grew as well: it was up to $71.8 billion in 2011 from $30.4 billion four years earlier. This made it the most expensive part of the 2008 farm bill,

262 Ben Senauer, "The Role of Food Stamps in the Recession," Federal Reserve Bank of Boston, Fall 2012, http://www.bos.frb.org/commdev/c&b/2012/fall/role-of-food-stamps-in-the-recession.htm.

and would have made it the most expensive part of the 2013 farm bill in the House of Representatives, until a controversial vote on July 11.[263]

In an attempt to cut this year's budget deficit, House Republicans sought to separate the SNAP program from the rest of the farm bill. This after a failed vote to pass a farm bill a month earlier, which would have cut food stamps by $20 billion over 10 years.[264] Despite these cuts, Republicans cited the extensive cost of food stamps in that bill as the primary reason for it failure, and said that the new arrangement—with SNAP funded under a separate law entirely—would facilitate debate on a progran they see as too expensive. For their part, Democrats in the House and Senators of both parties largely criticized the move, saying it left food stamp users too vulnerable to huge cuts. Politically, SNAP is a big reason why the Farm Bill passes through Congress so easily every five years. "The farm bill is a societal contract between urban and rural areas," said Dr. Carl Zulauf, an agricultural economist at The Ohio State University, in an interview with ARUSA.[265] Dr. Zulauf is referring to the political support the bill musters by appealing to people both from rural areas, which would benefit from farm subsidies, and urban areas, which benefit more from the SNAP program.

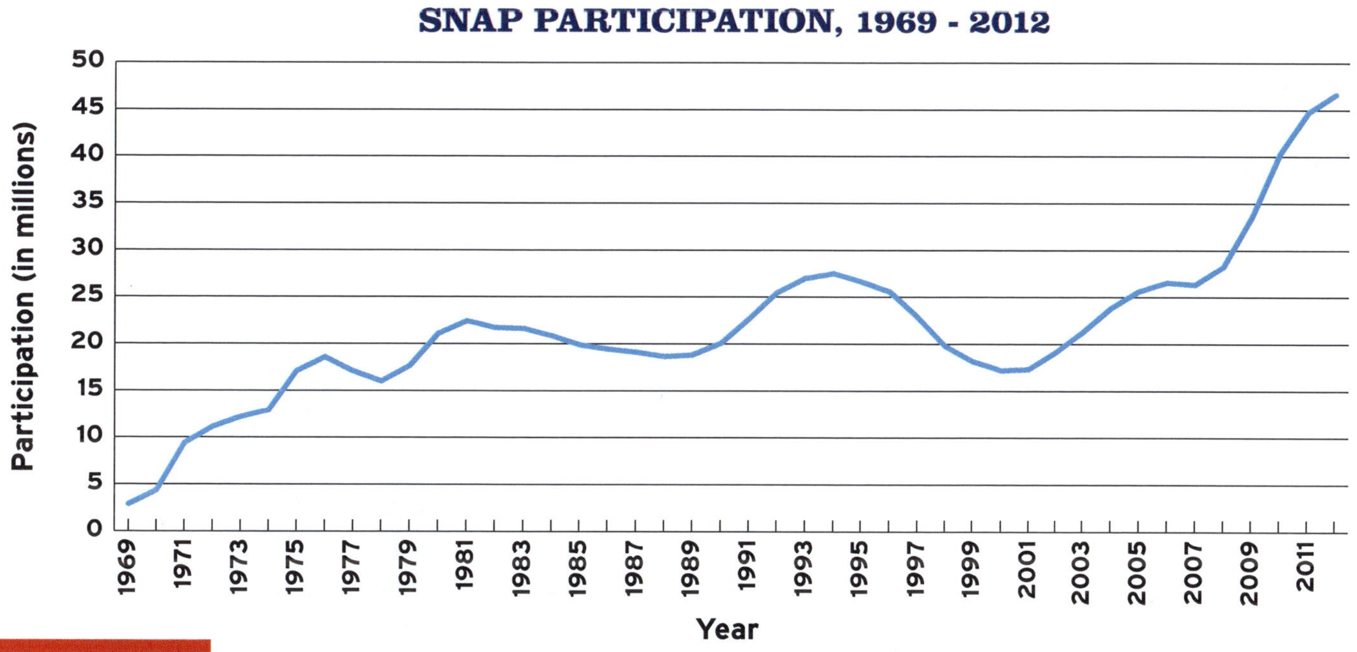

FIGURE 41 SOURCE: Department of Agriculture Food and Nutrition Service, http://www.fns.usda.gov/pd/SNAPsummary.htm.

This controversy around the debt impact of the farm bill begs an analysis of just how much the bill actually costs the American people. The most recent farm bill, passed in 2008, contained 15 different sections. Their descriptions and individual burden on the deficit (their cost) is listed below:

263 Jonathan Wesman and Ron Nixon, "House Republicans Push Through Farm Bill, Without Food Stamps," *New York Times*, July 11, 2013, http://www.nytimes.com/2013/07/12/us/politics/house-bill-would-split-farm-and-food-stamp-programs.html.

264 Nadia Arumugam, "Republicans Cut Food Stamps from the Farm Bill, so What's the Big Deal?" *Forbes*, July 13, 2013, http://www.forbes.com/sites/nadiaarumugam/2013/07/13/republicans-cut-food-stamps-from-farm-bill-whats-the-big-deal/.

265 Carl Zulauf, interivew by author, September 10, 2013.

TABLE 5 - TEN YEAR COST BASED ON 2008 FARM BILL	
Program	Estimated Costs Under Farm Bill (billions of dollars)
Commodities	$74.8
Conservation	$57.7
Crop Insurance	$61.6
Agricultural Trade Programs, Horticulture and Organic Spending, Supplemental Disaster Assistance	$7.1
Nutrition	$441.8
Other Spending	-$3
Total	**$640**
SOURCE: United States Department of Agriculture Economic Research Service, http://www.ers.usda.gov/topics/farm-economy/farm-commodity-policy/program-provisions/cost-of-2008-farm-bill.aspx#.UiIL72TXg0N.	

Note that the largest expenditure in the farm bill doesn't necessarily have to do with agriculture: "Nutrition" refers to the SNAP food stamp program, "WIC," or support for Women, Infants and Children, and other similar USDA programs. Three additional programs split up most of the remaining costs pretty evenly.

"Conservation" is exactly what it sounds like. The USDA website explains that this money goes towards "conservation through land retirement, farmland protection, and stewardship of land and water resources." "Crop Insurance" is government-supported private insurance in case a given farmer's crop is affected by some external event, mainly weather conditions. There has been plenty of talk in and out of the agricultural community saying that crop insurance is inefficient, because the government subsidized premiums and allows farmers to buy "Cadillac" insurance. Bob Young, chief economist with the Farm Bureau (an agricultural lobby) doesn't agree: "[The average farmer] is going to have to take a 25-30 yield hit before the checks or payments ever kick in," he told ARUSA in an interview, "so the notion that farmers are gaming the system…you might be able to game it one year, but you can't game it two years."[266]

The cost for "Commodities" is more complicated, because it goes to the heart of the farm bill's original purpose. In order to keep food, or commodity, prices low, decades ago Congress decided to assure farmers that no matter what market prices were, they would receive decent prices for their harvest, even if the government itself needed to pay those prices. This assurance served as a safety valve against plummeting crop prices: if farmers knew they would be paid by the government when prices dipped below a certain level, they felt less of a need to grow excess crops, the normal defense against a bad market. This practice continues today. Critics, such as Christian Cox, senior vice president of the Environmental Working Group, points out that these commodity payments to farmers are a bad deal for taxpayers. "The expensive cost of these programs is really cutting into our ability to fund other parts of the farm program, such as research, conservation, and rural development," he told the *Christian Science Monitor.*[267] Even if the intent of subsidies is to keep prices low for consumers, the tax dollars given to farms can be seen as a waste of money. This argument is strengthened by the fact that most farmland in the United States today is owned by large corporations, not the small, independent farms of yesteryear.

266 Bob Young, interview with author, September 12, 2013.
267 Richard Mertens, "Senate's new farm bill will waste billions on subsidies, critics say," *Christian Science Monitor*, June 10, 2013, http://www.csmonitor.com/USA/Politics/2013/0610/Senate-s-new-farm-bill-will-waste-billions-on-subsidies-critics-say.

A Congress Divided

As of writing, there are two different versions of the farm bill being debated. The Agriculture Reform, Food and Jobs Act of 2013 passed the Senate on June 10, 2013. The Senate farm bill would cost nearly $1 trillion over 10 years. It keeps food stamps as a provision, instead of setting SNAP aside as a separate matter, and this makes up a large percentage of its cost. It's a far more traditional farm bill than the current House bill, and it's useful in seeing just what makes up the USDA's largest funding source. Most importantly, it can tell us something about the farm bill's place in American political culture: in nearly every economic analysis of the bill, budgetary impact is measured not in the amount it will cost, but in the difference in cost from previous legislation. The Senate's 2013 farm bill, for example, spends $760 billion in nutrition programs over 10 years. But for many legislators, it's just as important that it spends $4 billion less over 10 years than the "CBO baseline," or the Congressional Budget Office's estimation of what we would spend if we renewed the status quo. This is a common feature in recurring budgetary laws: changes and trends in the budget are as important to observe as the total costs of its provisions.

An important feature of the Senate farm bill is its shift away from what are called "direct payments" to farmers. Direct payments are just that—paying farmers regardless of how much they grow, whether or not their crops contribute to the SNAP program or any other yardstick for national utility. In essence, direct payments just give money to farmers for, well, being farmers. The Environmental Working Group, which staunchly opposes the payments, pointed out in a report that they often benefit wealthy farmers the most.[268] In lieu of these direct payments, the Senate's farm bill places a greater priority on subsidizing farm insurance, although subsidies were cut for farmers making over $750,000 a year.[269 270]

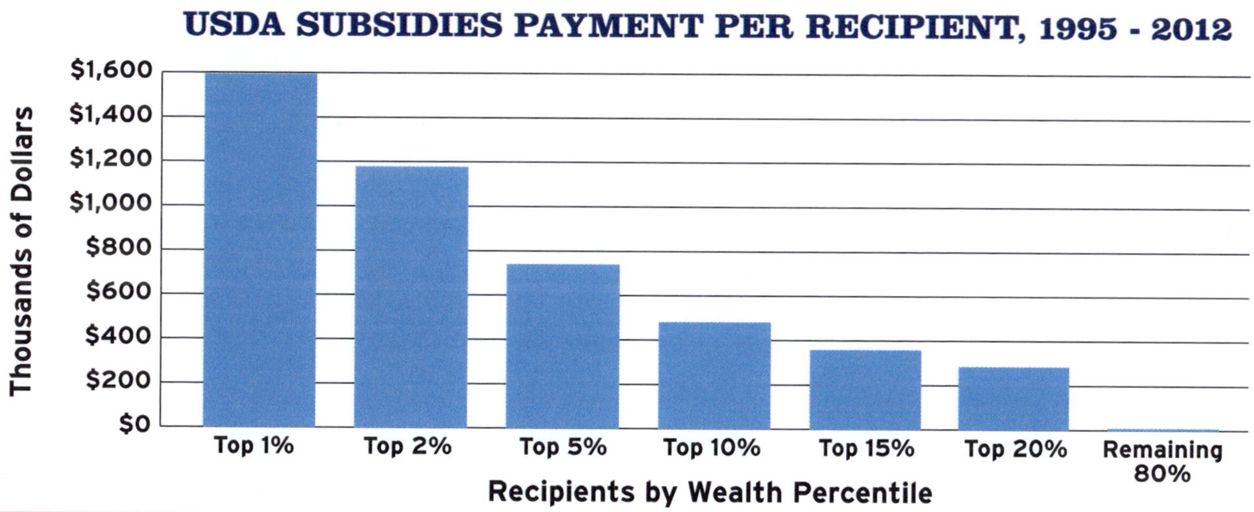

FIGURE 42 SOURCE: Environmental Working Group, http://farm.ewg.org/progdetail.php?fips=00000&progcode=total&page=conc&regionname=theUnitedStates.

The House, when it failed to pass a more traditional farm bill earlier this summer, opened itself up for a valuable experiment in politics: what happens when the most conventionally bipartisan (for better or worse) bill in Congress

268 Environmental Working Group, "Subsidizing High-Income Farms," Environmental Working Group, September 26, 2011, http://www.ewg.org/agmag/2011/09/subsidizing-high-income-farms.

269 Ramsey Cox, "Senate Passes Farm Bill in 66-27 Vote," The Hill, June 10, 2013, http://thehill.com/blogs/floor-action/senate/304585-senate-votes-66-27-to-pass-a-five-year-farm-bill.

270 Environmental Working Group, "USDA subsidies in the United States totaled $292.5 billion from 1995-2012," http://farm.ewg.org/progdetail.php?fips=00000&progcode=total&page=conc&regionname=theUnitedStates.

doesn't get the votes in needs? The microscopes of the Washington beltway, specifically those of far left and right think tanks, have fallen squarely on agricultural policy.

Conservative groups like the Heritage Foundation point out that separating the farm bill from food stamp funding would make it easier to debate the economic and social details of the latter. Still, the House GOP's farm bill itself is still wasteful, given the large government subsidy of crop insurance for farmers that might not require it.[271] For Heritage and similar think tanks, the farm bill represents the worst of American budgetary policy: pulling a fast one on the American people by passing a huge spending bill without leaving time for a substantial debate, and leaning towards the will of powerful special interests groups such as the agricultural lobby. There was a special animosity this legislative session for the idea (though it probably won't be in the final bill) that the farm bill could pass as a permanent bill, instead of having to be renewed every five years, thus making permanent the perceived errors in policy.

For liberals, the separation of the SNAP program from the general House farm bill represented a grave threat to the poor. Even though House Republicans said they would write a new SNAP bill as soon as the farm bill was passed, Democrats didn't take the offer seriously. Since then, Democrats and the President have been adamant that the farm bill will not pass both houses without nutrition assistance included.[272]

What Now?

Given the degree of gridlock in Congress, the chance of reconciliation on a compromise farm bill appears quite low at time of writing. Yet, regardless of the political setting, the budgetary issues put forward in the farm bill debate are complex ones: How connected should nutrition assistance be to agricultural subsidies and insurance? How should the government price its commodity supports? Should farmers receive direct payments at all? These are complicated questions that will no doubt be the subject of interest group lobbying and constituent pressure alike. Ultimately, the most difficult aspect of the farm bill, like many aspects of federal government, is just how big it should be. After the billions of dollars it spends annually are in the hands of families and organizations across the country, one thing is clear: this mammoth piece of legislation doesn't get nearly the popular attention, or the political scrutiny, that it deserves.

★

271 Amy Payne, "Morning Bell: Late Night Shenanigans in the House," heritage.org, July 11, 2013, http://blog.heritage.org/2013/07/11/morning-bell-late-night-farm-bill-shenanigans-in-the-house/.

272 Michael McAuliff, Sabrina Siddiqui, Arthur Delaney, "Food Stamp Cuts Derail Farm Bill," The *Huffington Post*, June 20, 2013, http://www.huffingtonpost.com/2013/06/20/food-stamp-cuts_n_3474102.html.

APPENDIX I: Index of Figures and Tables

FIGURES

America's Finances

Social Insurance and Safety Net

Foreign Relations and Security

APPENDIX I: Index of Figures and Tables

Education, Science, & Technology

Agriculture

TABLES

America's Finances

Social Insurance and Safety Net

Foreign Relations and Security

Agriculture

APPENDIX II: List of Useful Links

ARUSA SPONSORS

American Education Foundation
http://www.americafound.org/

Institute of Politics at Harvard University
http://www.iop.harvard.edu/

Harvard Political Review
http://www.harvardpolitics.com/

U.S. FEDERAL GOVERNMENT

Congressional Budget Office
http://www.cbo.gov/

Government Accountability Office
http://www.gao.gov/

Joint Committee on Taxation
http://www.jct.gov/

Office of Management and Budget
http://www.whitehouse.gov/omb

President's Budget Requests ("Budget of the U.S. Government")
http://www.gpo.gov/fdsys/browse/collectionGPO.action?collectionCode=BUDGET

INDEPENDENT RESEARCH ORGANIZATIONS

Center on Budget and Policy Priorities
http://www.cbpp.org/

The Hamilton Project (Brookings Institution)
http://www.hamiltonproject.org/

Tax Policy Center (Brookings Institution and Urban Institute)
http://www.taxpolicycenter.org/

Printed in Dunstable, United Kingdom

91218890R00051